CONCORDIA UNIVERSITY

3 4211 00138 2954

Y0-ARW-953

Infants and Toddlers:
A Resource Guide
for Practitioners

Infants and Toddlers: A Resource Guide for Practitioners

Edited by

Michael Bender, EdD
Vice President of Educational Programs
The Kennedy Institute

Professor of Education
The Johns Hopkins University

Joint Appointment
The Johns Hopkins School of Medicine
Baltimore, Maryland

Carol Ann Baglin, MEd, MA
Director
Maryland Infants and Toddlers Program
Baltimore, Maryland

SINGULAR PUBLISHING GROUP, INC.
San Diego, California

KLINCK MEMORIAL LIBRARY
Concordia University
River Forest, IL 60305-1499

Singular Publishing Group, Inc.
4284 41st Street
San Diego, California 92105-1197

©1992 by Singular Publishing Group, Inc.

All rights, including that of translation reserved. No part of this publication
may by reproduced, stored in a retrieval system, or transmitted in any form or
by any means, electronic, mechanical, recording, or otherwise, without the prior
written permission of the publisher.

Typeset by So Cal Graphics
Text typeset in 10/12 Times Roman;
    display set in Helvetica.

Printed by McNaughton & Gunn

Library of Congress Cataloging-in-Publication Data

Bender, Michael, 1943-
        Infants and toddlers : a resource guide for practitioners /
    Michael Bender, Carol Ann Baglin.
                p. cm.
    Includes bibliographical references and index.
    ISBN 1-879105-36-5
    1. Handicapped children—Rehabilitation. 2. Handicapped
    children—Services for. I. Baglin, Carol Ann. II. Title.
    [DNLM: 1. Child Care—organization & administration. 2. Child
    development Disorders—prevention & control. 3. Child Health
    Services—organization & administration. 4. Family Health.
    5. Infant Care—organization & administration. WS 350.6 B458i]
    RJ138.B45 1992
    362.1'9892—dc20
    DNLM/DLC
    for Library of Congress   91-5184
                                                                                   CIP

Printed in the United States of America

To my original infants and toddlers—Stephen, Andrew, and Sydney Amanda, with all my love.

M. B.

For the three loveliest smiles in my life—my children, Sarabeth, Samantha, and Seth.

C. A. B.

CONTENTS

CONTRIBUTORS

Noma B. Anderson, PhD
Associate Professor
Department Chairperson
Department of Communications,
    Sciences, and Disorders
Howard University
Washington, DC

Carol Ann Baglin, MEd, MA
Special Educator and Marriage and
    Family Counselor
Director, Maryland Infants and Toddlers
    Program
Office for Children, Youth, and Families
Baltimore, Maryland

Michael Bender, EdD
Vice President of Educational Programs
The Kennedy Institute
Professor of Education
The Johns Hopkins University
Joint Appointment
The Johns Hopkins School of Medicine
Baltimore, Maryland

Nancy Donohue Colletta, PhD
Clinically Oriented Developmental
    Psychologist
Center for Infant Study
University of Maryland School of
    Medicine
Baltimore, Maryland

Michael A. Gilbert, MA
Technical Assistance Specialist
Maryland Infants and Toddlers Program
Office for Children, Youth, and Families
Baltimore, Maryland

Barbara Hanft, MA, OTR/L, FAOTA
Consultant/Lecturer
Silver Spring, Maryland

Susan N. Hochberg, MS
Family Coordinator
Maryland Infants and Toddlers Program
Office for Children, Youth, and Families
Baltimore, Maryland

Lemmietta G. McNeilly, MA
Doctoral Student
Coordinator, Speech and Language
    Clinic
Department of Communications,
    Sciences, and Disorders
Howard University
Washington, DC

William G. Sciarillo, ScD, MSN
Advisor for Community Health
    Resources Development
Children's Medical Services
Maryland Department of Health and
    Mental Hygiene
Baltimore, Maryland

Janeen M. Taylor, PhD
The Johns Hopkins University
Maryland Infants and Toddlers Program
Office for Children, Youth, and Families
Baltimore, Maryland

Deborah L. Von Rembow, MA, EdS
Resource Development Specialist
Maryland Infants and Toddlers Program
Office for Children, Youth, and Families
Baltimore, Maryland

ACKNOWLEDGMENTS

We would like to acknowledge, with special thanks, the many professionals who provided information and special expertise, especially from the Office of Special Education Programs (OSEP) at the U. S. Department of Education, the National Early Childhood Technical Assistance System (NEC*TAS), the Council for Exceptional Children (CEC), the National Center for Clinical Infant Programs (NCCIP), the Association for the Care of Children's Health (ACCH), and the Mid South Regional Resource Center (MSRRC). In addition, the many publications from the Carolina Policy Institute were of assistance in their overall assessment of how states are implementing Part H.

We also would like to acknowledge Larry Edelman of Project Copernicus, Jane Headings, Linda O'Mara, and staff members from the Kennedy Institute in Baltimore, Maryland for their input and technical assistance, and Kim McCrae and Sherea Makle from the Lending Interdisciplinary Multimedia Resource Center, for their help in locating many fine resources. Also, we would like to thank Marlene Marrinaccio of the Baltimore City Infants and Toddlers Program, Baltimore City Health Department, Carolyn Savage who provided professional support, and Michael Argentino for his patient and careful support in copying the many materials needed for this resource. Finally, our heartfelt thanks go to the members of the Family Support Network for their overall guidance in developing a family centered system.

PREFACE

Infants and Toddlers: A Resouce Guide for Practitioners and Families
was originally conceived by the authors when Public Law 99-457, Part H,
was in its first year of planning. At that time, most professionals, although concerned about funding issues, were still optimistic about the
promise the new legislation had for an under-served population of children with disabilities and their families.

During that time, both authors, having had lengthy teaching and clinical experiences with children and families, felt the need to address in
writing, some of the pressing questions that were beginning to surface as
a result of this legislation. As a State Director of Infants and Toddlers
Program and a Chair of a State Interagency Coordinating Council, the
authors knew the same questions were being asked nationally.

To gain a cross section of these most asked questions, it became paramount to interview parents, professionals, related service staff, agency
representatives, and advocates. These individuals were asked to help the
authors plan a resource of ideas and information which they felt would be
helpful and could be used as a guide for those entering the early intervention field. While initially the resource was to be a cookbook of ideas, it
quickly became apparent that what was really needed were discussions
and practical recommendations in areas associated with infants and toddlers that were not widely known. For example, the mental health needs
of infants and their families was a growing concern to practitioners and
clinic personnel. However, this area was little known to school systems or
professionals, who had minimum training in infant mental health. Serving special populations by understanding their customs or mores, specifically as it relates to the roles of parents and families, was a growing
problem in urban and ethnic parts of communities, but not widely understood by the professionals providing early intervention services.

Although this legislation was developed as a family centered interagency initiative, the authors became acutely aware of the lack of "typical
parent" input on local and some state interagency coordinating councils
throughout the country. It was obvious that most parents with infants
and toddlers with disabilities had their own daily crises, and sharing their
concerns and questions with others on a committee or council, would
have to wait. For most of these parents, daily survival was both their
immediate and long-term goal. As a result, the authors interviewed par-

ents of specific-needs children, and selected one to write the chapter on family issues and concerns. This parent also served as the Family Coordinator for a state's Infant and Toddler Program.

Other areas that created major information and resource concerns involved service coordination or case management, as well as how one prepares practitioners to provide early intervention services. These areas became the thrust for how one could effectively find and manage interagency resources. All of these concerns were developed into chapters and written by the professionals most experienced in addressing these complex issues.

An area often unnoticed, but singled out time and again by parents, was their need for information concerning the provision of early intervention services in child-care settings. Recent publicity about the lack of appropriate infant and toddler care, as well as the abuses regularly being exposed in day-care settings, has escalated these concerns to the top of most parents' fears. Information contained in this particular chapter is important reading and details the issues one must consider before accepting the day-care option.

A final step in the evolution of this resource was defining the individuals we hoped would read this information. It was widely agreed by those interviewed, that the authors and contributors could not discuss all areas of early intervention. In fact, books, journals, and articles addressing areas such as assessment, family service plans, and interagency team building were already beginning to proliferate in early intervention libraries. Initially, "hands-on" early interventionists and parents were viewed as being the primary market that could benefit from this resource. However, it quickly became clear by the time the last chapters were completed, that administrators, coordinators, and those providing technical assistance to families also could benefit from this information.

There was also a realization that funding for infant and toddler programs was going to be difficult. Thus, this resource was designed to start most individuals on their way by providing necessary and practical information that could be used to support or develop their own programs. Listings of resources and recommendations were added to allow them to move at their own pace in following up or expanding their informational base. Of paramount importance was that information, although generic in some instances, be as current as possible and reflect best practice methodology or suggestions.

Because the authors are involved daily in the struggle to implement infant and toddler legislation, it is their hope that this resource be more than another text in the ever increasing early childhood domain. The practitioners who have written it, the reviewers who have added to it, and the parents who live it, see this information being useful for courses, workshops, inservice programs, and other types of training. Whoever participates in these types of instructions should be acutely aware that new issues will replace existing concerns, but some problems (like funding) will always remain. The bantering of who does what, and who funds what, are indeed critical issues that must be equitably resolved by those charged with this responsibility. However, it is important to not forget that children with special needs and disabilities are being born every day, and their families are awaiting services. If these infants and toddlers are to be provided the opportunity to function effectively in their environment, they will require help and expertise from all disciplines, professionals, and agencies.

INTRODUCTION

In 1986, Congress passed Public Law 99-457 (P. L. 99-457) which became known as the 1986 Amendments to the Education of the Handicapped Act (EHA). With these amendments, and the establishment of a new Part H of the Act, a nationwide effort was started in which states were given 5 years to develop and implement multidisciplinary, interagency programs of early intervention services for handicapped infants and toddlers and their families. These programs, known as "Part H" programs, were to be comprehensive and coordinated statewide, and by the fifth year, they were to become an entitlement. That is, all eligible infants and toddlers, and their families would have a right to early intervention services through an individualized family service plan (IFSP), and not just to those services that happen to be available in the community.

In 1991, the 101st Congress reauthorized the Education of the Handicapped Act, and the resulting legislation, Public Law 101-476, changed the name of the Education of the Handicapped Act to the Individuals with Disabilities Education Act (IDEA).

As a result of this change, the term "handicap" was replaced with the term "disability" and the language of the act was translated into "people first language." Today, handicapped infants and toddlers are referred to as "infants and toddlers with disabilities."

On October 7, 1991, Part H was reauthorized by the United States Congress. Consequently, the "Individuals with Disabilities Education Act Amendments of 1991" is known as P.L. 102-119. Additional early intervention services were included, such as assistive technology devices and services, vision services, and transportation. Early intervention personnel were expanded to include family therapists, orientation and mobility specialists, and pediatricians and other physicians.

For some professionals, especially those residing in states that were previously mandated by state legislation to provide infant and toddler services (birth mandate states), the legislation was viewed initially as a way of supporting and expanding much needed programs. Funding was expected to flow through a reordering or reallocating of existing state and local resources, although initial discussions between federal and state authorities failed to clarify just how this was to be accomplished. Many of these original local and state fiscal concerns continue to exist today and have had a negative impact on the full implementation of the law.

Because of a continual need for practical information in this area of disability, *Infants and Toddlers: A Resource Guide for Practitioners and Families* was developed. It was conceptualized to serve as a resource for individuals newly entering the infant and toddler intervention field, as well as for those practitioners who work daily in agencies or provider systems. It also attempts to address many family concerns that are often left unanswered as a result of the time consuming and crisis nature of parenting an infant or toddler with disabilities.

Early intervention in the context of this resource is viewed as a process that begins at referral and ends as a child is transitioned at age three to special education, Head Start, community preschools, or child-care programs. For example, a primary referral source such as a pediatrician, child-care provider, nurse, or parent may be concerned about the development of an infant or toddler. At this point, a referral can be made to a "child find" contact within the community. Relevant records, including health and medical reports, previous assessments, and developmental screenings are reviewed. In some instances, an infant or toddler with possible developmental delay or with an established condition likely to result in delay, may require specific evaluations to determine eligibility. With this information, and input from the parent, an individualized family service plan (IFSP) is developed and a case manager or service coordinator is identified. The IFSP is reviewed within 6 months and updated as necessary. When an infant or toddler approaches age three, a transition plan is developed to identify his or her next program. Figure I-1 illustrates the referral to transition process.

The eight chapters in this resource have been written by clinicians, professionals, and parents who interact daily with infants and toddlers. Their expertise is highly regarded and well known, because most serve as National consultants to states seeking practical information for implementing early intervention programs. The common thread among these contributors is their willingness to share ideas and go beyond their agency or discipline boundaries, as they attempt to seek answers to complex questions. In addition, the authors interviewed numerous parents and professionals from health, mental health, education, and social services to find out their perspectives and to elicit questions they felt needed further clarification.

The following chapters articulate a summation of the critical topics in need of discussion at this time in early intervention implementation. Many of these areas and topics will inexorably be replaced by others, as time goes by. Many, however, will need to be continually revisited as funding streams change and target populations are revised.

Chapter 1, written by Barbara Hanft and Deborah Von Rembow, addresses "The Individualized Family Service Plan Process." It includes an

Figure I-1
Referral to transition process

EARLY INTERVENTION PROCESS

PROCESS FLOW

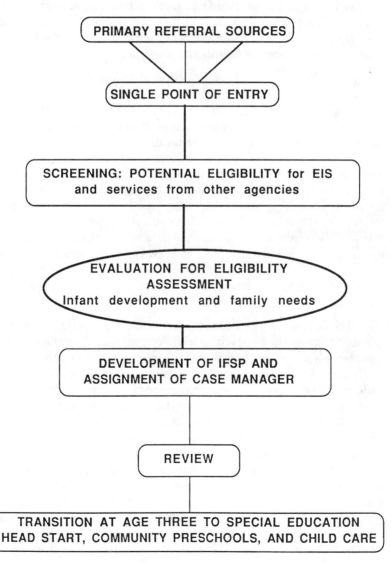

PRIMARY REFERRAL SOURCES

SINGLE POINT OF ENTRY

SCREENING: POTENTIAL ELIGIBILITY for EIS
and services from other agencies

EVALUATION FOR ELIGIBILITY
ASSESSMENT
Infant development and family needs

DEVELOPMENT OF IFSP AND
ASSIGNMENT OF CASE MANAGER

REVIEW

TRANSITION AT AGE THREE TO SPECIAL EDUCATION
HEAD START, COMMUNITY PRESCHOOLS, AND CHILD CARE

overview of the Individualized Family Service Plan (IFSP) and the foundations for collaboration necessary as one develops partnerships between family members and professionals. A section on communication and collaboration, listening skills, and open-ended questions where families are asked to describe their concerns, feelings, and ideas demonstrates how to bring families into the process of working with professionals. Using family assessment techniques and instruments to identify family resources and priorities, comprises an important component of this chapter, as it directly relates to the development, implementation, and evaluation of the IFSP. The chapter also includes a sample completed IFSP. In addition, Appendix A offers a resource list of selected instruments for identifying family resources, concerns, and priorities.

Chapter 2, written by Nancy Colletta, discusses the "Mental Health Needs of Infants and their Families." The chapter initially provides the reader with some general assumptions about the emotional development of infants and toddlers and moves quickly into identifying the escalating infant mental health problem. Colletta offers a list of characteristics of infants who are at high risk for difficulties in emotional development and then provides intervention suggestions for temperamentally difficult children. A second component of the chapter addresses the needs of drug-exposed babies, followed by suggested intervention strategies and informational resources readers will be able to use for their specific programs. Colletta also describes and suggests interventions for abused and neglected infants and those who have parents with serious social and emotional problems. The chapter concludes with information on some models of intervention and a discussion of infants, who despite overwhelming odds, grow up to function as adaptive and stable adults.

Chapter 3, written by Noma Anderson and Lemmietta McNeilly, addresses "Meeting the Needs of Special Populations." This timely chapter discusses what is meant by culturally diverse in terms of cultural beliefs and values. This information is especially important for those working with special population parents, in that the philosophy of early intervention is predominantly based on a view that considers the present as preparation for the future. In contrast, the authors describe many special population families as sharing a cultural orientation in which the present is viewed as a consequence of the past. In essence, these families have greater confidence in following tradition, which often is tied to fatalistic (it is God's will) beliefs. This situation can create problems for how one works with special population parents and how the early intervention process is presented. Information is also provided on how one targets services to lower income families and how the health care system appears so very different to them. The chapter concludes with a discussion of

HIV-positive infants and their families, the barriers to their integration of services, and the needs of practitioners who serve HIV-infected children and their families.

Chapter 4, written by Michael Gilbert, William Sciarillo, and Deborah Von Rembow, explores the issue of "Service Coordination Through Case Management." Initially, the reader is familiarized with the functions of a case manager as detailed in the federal regulations. This familiarization includes explaining how the performance of evaluation and assessments are coordinated, how one facilitates and participates in the development, review, and evaluation of individualized family service plans, assisting families in identifying available service providers. The authors also define advocacy services and how to coordinate medical and health providers and the development of a transition plan. A second part of this chapter describes the events that happen as part of the care coordination process. This description includes the stages of engagement, discovery, implementation, review, and disengagement. A final part of the chapter presents a description of existing types of resources that are available in one state, which may be available to them. Issues for agencies providing case management conclude this chapter.

Chapter 5 was written by Susan Hochberg, who as a parent of a child with disabilities has survived the process of living with crisis and searching for appropriate resources. Through her chapter "A Parent's Perspective: Empowering the Family" she explains her feelings of disappointment, fear, guilt, and anger after there is a realization of her situation. She stresses the need for "family centered care" and lists the changes that are required to move from a child-centered service delivery system to one that has a family centered focus. The chapter provides examples of how to motivate and empower a family so they will feel part of the early intervention process. Hochberg discusses the value of parent support services and resources and the difficult and stressful problems that surface as a result of interacting with professionals.

Chapter 6, written by Janeen Taylor, discusses "Preparing Practitioners for Early Intervention Services." In this chapter, Taylor initially discusses the preparation and need for ongoing education of individuals providing early intervention services. She clarifies why traditional definitions for children who are disabled are inappropriate for young children because there are few if any accurate predictors of later developmental status. For those new to the training area, Taylor describes what constitutes a state's Comprehensive System of Personnel Development (CSPD) and the elements that define it. She concludes her chapter by citing other avenues for developing early intervention competencies and the continual importance to conduct and tie needs assessments to inservice education, professional development, and technical assistance.

Chapter 7, written by Carol Ann Baglin, addresses the critical and timely issue of "Implementing Early Intervention in a Child-Care Setting." The introduction of this chapter presents a description of different types of child-care settings and identifies some existing federal funding sources for child care. Central to the chapter, however, is information about regulations, standards, and the quality issues required if one is to carefully choose child care. In this day of questionable child-care practices, the author lists invaluable questions everyone should ask when seeking day care for their child. Baglin infers that by not asking these questions you may be exposing young children to neglect or abuse. This chapter concludes with a discussion on the need for integrated child-care settings that can provide comprehensive programs for educational and therapeutic interventions in a developmentally appropriate environment.

Chapter 8, written by Carol Ann Baglin, brings together information on "Managing Interagency Resources." It presents the family, who in most instances knows most about their child, as the primary care provider. For those readers not used to working with or interacting on an interagency level, this chapter describes how health, human service agencies, and education have similar goals for serving infants and toddlers, but different approaches. Interagency collaboration goals such as prevention, early identification, referral, screening, eligibility determination, assessment, and individualized family service plans are discussed as well as the activities that are common to the different interagency service programs. A final section includes information on how to develop interagency agreements and the sharing of financial resources. Finally, suggestions are given on how to identify funding resources, as well as information on how to assess the progress of their early intervention system. This information should prove valuable to those who wish to understand the complex process of managing interagency resources.

Resource Appendices A,B,C,D, and E, which address Assessment Instruments, Child-Care Questions, Early Intervention Services, Interagency Agreements, and Federally Funded Early Intervention Programs, are provided as additional information for the reader who may have interests in these specific areas.

Chapter 1

The Individualized Family Service Plan Process

BARBARA HANFT
DEBORAH L. VON REMBOW

The impetus for Public Law 99-457 grew out of an extended consumer/ advocacy movement for individuals with disabilities during the 1960s and 1970s (Hanft, 1991; Pizzo, 1983) and a recognition that providing early intervention services to children would benefit society by:

- Enhancing the development of young children with disabilities and minimizing their potential for developmental delay.
- Reducing the cost to society of providing special education and related services when children enter school.
- Minimizing institutionalization and maximizing the child's potential for independent living.
- Supporting families in meeting the special needs of their infants and toddlers with disabilities. [P. L. 99-457, Sec. 671 (a)]

Literature in the 1980s supported these views and emphasized early childhood development as being an interactive process between child and environment (Smolak, 1986), which provides a framework for a family centered approach to early intervention. The emphasis on family was significant, because historically parents were portrayed as uneducated or

1

unable to make decisions regarding their child's care solely on the basis that their child had a disability. At best, parents were viewed as well intentioned but passive and unable to make appropriate decisions regarding their children's well-being (Blacher, 1982; Lipsky, 1985; Murphy, 1982; Pizzo, 1983; Travis, 1976; Versluys, 1980). Thus, early intervention services were directed *at* parents to train or educate them to carry out home programs or other interventions prescribed by the experts (Bazyk, 1989; Powell, 1988).

Currently, early intervention specialists and family members are viewed differently. Most parents are recognized as resourceful and competent in making decisions about early intervention services that will affect their own and their children's lives (Allen & Hudd, 1987; Pizzo, 1990; Seitz & Provence, 1990). Professionals now have new roles as collaborators and partners with families, who are viewed as resourceful team members rather than merely recipients of a team's services (Anderson & Hinojosa, 1984; Dunst, Trivette, & Deal, 1988; Hanft, 1989; Miller, Lynch, & Campbell, 1990; Shelton, Jeppson, & Johnson, 1987).

The early intervention provisions of P. L. 99-457 clearly suggest the family's central role in caring for their children with disabilities. The requirement that early intervention services be provided to eligible infants and toddlers and their families in conformity with an *Individualized Family Service Plan (IFSP)* highlights the necessity for a family context in comprehensive service delivery systems. Indeed, the federal regulations stipulate that "the plan must be developed jointly by the family and appropriate qualified personnel," and "must include services necessary to enhance the development of the child and the capacity of the family to meet the special needs of the child" (34 CFR 303.340).

Further, the regulations mandate timelines within which the IFSP must be developed, reviewed, and evaluated, and stipulate the participants in IFSP meetings, as well as specifying the content of the IFSP. What neither the statute nor regulations suggest, however, is the process by which all of these actions should occur prior to documenting decisions on a written plan within 45 calendar days of referral to the early intervention system.

OVERVIEW OF THE INDIVIDUALIZED FAMILY SERVICE PLAN

A family-centered approach to early intervention not only recognizes that infants and toddlers with special needs live within family structures and communities and are dependent on adults to meet their needs, but values and promotes family direction in all aspects of planning and delivering services. The IFSP process should provide a mechanism for building family and professional partnerships that enables families to make informed choices about the early intervention services they want for their children and themselves (Johnson, McGonigel, & Kaufmann, 1989). Thus, the IFSP *process* assumes greater significance than the resulting *document*, which should serve primarily as a written reflection of the information exchange between families and professionals, and subsequent decision-making by families. As stated in a document prepared by the Parents as Partners Project (1988) at Alta Mira Specialized Family Services Inc. and cited in Johnson, McGonigel, and Kaufmann (1989), "The IFSP is not just paperwork or evaluations that must be done so that your child can be enrolled in a program. The IFSP is a partnership that will last the entire time your child and family are with the early intervention program."

If the IFSP is a process that includes the writing of a document, then it is important to define the elements and describe the characteristics of the process that lead to the written confirmation of the collaborative effort. In 1989, Johnson, McGonigel, and Kaufmann identified a number of key activities that occur as part of the IFSP process regardless of program model. Identified elements, which some states have chosen to address in IFSP policy, include:

- First contact between a family and the early intervention system
- Assessment planning
- Child assessment
- Identification of family resources, priorities, and concerns
- Development of outcomes to meet identified child and family needs
- Implementation of the IFSP
- Formal and informal evaluation of the IFSP.

To effectively implement the IFSP process, early intervention systems must define procedures for each identified element. Maryland, for instance, has specified components for each step in the IFSP process that include timeline, purpose, individuals involved, individual(s) responsible, what happens and how, as well as decision options, procedural safeguards, and data collection requirements associated with the step. Such information provides clear direction for families and professionals and highlights the fluid nature of IFSP teams as well as the ongoing nature of the IFSP decision-making process.

For an IFSP to be *individualized* the process must be interactive and flexible, with individual family needs and preferences determining the dynamics. Progression through the steps may vary from sequential to simultaneous, depending on the unique circumstances of each child and family. Whatever the progression may be, the elements are interdependent, with information and activities occurring at various stages affecting each other (Johnson, McGonigel, & Kaufmann, 1989). The information exchange during the first contacts between family members and early intervention personnel not only shapes the evaluation and assessment process, but also initiates the identification of family resources, priorities, and concerns, and influences the relationships between parents and professionals throughout the family's involvement with the early intervention system.

This chapter discusses various elements of the IFSP process from the perspective of the interrelationships of components. Preliminary comments are directed to the concept of collaboration, which is the foundation on which all aspects of the IFSP process are built.

FOUNDATIONS FOR COLLABORATION

Establishing and maintaining partnerships between family members and professionals rests on fundamental principles and skills related to collaboration. Following is a list of operational principles and a discussion of strategic skills related to enhancing collaboration to promote informed decision-making throughout the IFSP process.

- Collaboration is the process of working together to achieve a common goal. It implies cooperation and teamwork between equal partners, that is, family members and professionals.
- Collaboration begins with the first family contact, when the process of identifying family resources, concerns, and priorities begins. It continues through planning, developing, providing, and evaluating the effectiveness of early intervention services.
- Collaboration includes mutual respect for cultural background, child-rearing practices and family routines and traditions.
- Collaboration is built on communication; communication is inextricably interwoven with values, attitudes, interests, and knowledge.

Cultural Diversity and Collaboration

In 1956, Margaret Mead described cultural differences as the "learned ways of a people . . . which cut across class, racial and religious lines" (p. 262). Sensitivity to and respect for the cultural values and customs of families are crucial to the success of the IFSP process. In addition to culture, the family's religious, ethnic, and racial backgrounds help define individual members' daily routines, traditions, and child-rearing practices. Cultural groups also hold diverse views about health care, education, and the affect of disability (see Chapter 3).

Families, or individuals within a family, may hold beliefs that do not coincide with those held by other members of their cultural group. For this reason, early intervention specialists must recognize that there is no single "correct" way to help families identify their resources, concerns, and priorities to develop outcomes, or to plan services. Hanson, Lynch, and Wayman (1990) observe that some individuals and families experience a strong cultural identification; others do not.

> Regardless of how strong or weak the identification appears to be, these values affect families' participation, beginning with the amount and type of participation (in early intervention) that they choose, goals they may select, and the family members who may be involved in intervention efforts. (p. 113)

It is helpful to keep in mind that culture exists on a continuum; an individual family may function at any point on this continuum (Vincent, Salisbury, Strain, McCormick, & Tessier, 1990). To develop realistic outcomes with families from diverse ethnic, racial, and cultural backgrounds, early intervention specialists must understand the family's beliefs and values.

Expectations that members of a particular age or cultural group would automatically prefer to meet early interventionists at home, for example, "because mothers usually don't work outside the home," sets up a barrier to identifying outcomes specific for each family. Because families with children who have special needs hold diverse views of the world, one formula for providing early intervention services to every family cannot be proposed.

The Affect of Professionals' Values on Collaboration

Professionals, as caregivers for children with special needs, must also consider how their own cultural values and beliefs affect their relationships with the families they serve. Differences in value systems between parents and professionals may result in interpretation of the professionals' behavior as being either helpful or interfering. According to Johnston (1980):

> This current dilemma in Western society (of interpreting professional behavior) has been brought about by our changing notions of what is considered, in the practice of modern medicine, to be the culturally correct approach in parenting behavior with often little regard to either the folk wisdom present in many groups or what rules are valued. (p. 12)

Professionals' attitudes and beliefs about family life create expectations for their role as service providers and influence how they think families "should behave." These attitudes and beliefs are formed by each person's experiences with his or her family of origin as well as the family formed as adults (Hanft, 1989). Such internalized values about what families should look like and how they should behave affect all personal and professional interactions (Duhl, 1983).

Margaret Mead (1956), writing for nurses about cultural diversity, urged them to watch their own culture as a way of sensitizing themselves to the cultural behavior of the people for whom they were caring.

> By emphasizing cultural differences . . . we enhance the dignity of each people, and we mute the types of judgement involved in political and religious differences . . . If the nurse is aware that she herself comes from a culture with a full set of cultural attitudes on every subject— from reward and punishment to the exact spot over which one should brush one's teeth—and learns to watch the ways in which she responds culturally (that is, with the same order of behavior as any other woman of her age, class, religion, education, and from her part of the country), this is half the battle. (p. 261)

Communication and Collaboration

Communication is the exchange of thoughts, messages, information and feelings between two or more people. Good communication skills are critical to the success of establishing a positive relationship with family members throughout the IFSP process.

Communication is the largest single factor affecting the relationships people form with one another. It covers a broad continuum of the ways people share information, feelings, and ideas (Satir, 1972). Communication includes verbal elements, or words, as well as the nonverbal messages expressed through body position, tone of voice, rate of breathing, facial expression, and gestures. *How* communication is accomplished is as important as *what* is communicated.

Listening skills also are an essential part of establishing partnerships because they convey respect and facilitate communication between colleagues. By listening and responding to what families say, professionals convey the attitude that "what you have to say is important." This is in contrast to hierarchical relationships where one party, the subordinate, listens and responds to an authority who gives directions.

Listening may be accomplished either actively or passively. The passive listener listens in relative silence but conveys an attitude of acceptance. During active listening, the professional expresses understanding of what the parent has said. This response provides an opportunity for the parent to verify or clarify the communication. The professional should always ask him- or herself, "What is this parent saying to me?" The desired outcome is for family members to feel that they are understood.

Focus groups with families emphasize the importance they place on how willing professionals are to invest time in developing rapport with them. Their comments suggest, at least in the early stages of adjusting to the child's disability, that families may need specialists who can provide both formal and informal functions, for example, who are both knowledgeable and emotionally responsive (Summers, et al, in press).

Open-ended questions invite family members to describe their concerns, feelings, and ideas in their own terms. For example, asking "How do mealtimes go for Julie?" rather than "Can Julie hold her own cup?" or "Does she use a spoon?" gives the family an opportunity to describe how they see Julie's behavior. Open-ended questions invite more than a yes or no answer. Likewise, asking "What seems most important to you right now?" rather than recommending that Julie hold her own cup gives family members a chance to choose an outcome that is important to them.

In contrast, close-ended questions can be answered only by a limited response, which tends to shut down the communication process if used too often. Such questions focus on topics of interest to the professional, rather than following up on concerns raised by the parent.

Open-ended questions provide four main functions when used during the IFSP process:

1. They *invite comments* from family members without limiting what they may want to say or express, for example, "Tell me about your concerns for Steven?"
2. They encourage family members to *elaborate on a point*, for example, "What else would you like Steven to learn about right now?"
3. They can help *describe an action or behavior* more specifically, for example, "What are you hoping therapy will help Steven do?"
4. They can *focus and clarify family member's actions and priorities*, for example, "What do you do when Steven only sleeps for two hours at a time?" or "What would help you catch up on your sleep?"

The extensive use of close-ended questions or checklists, particularly if questions are asked in sequential order, inhibits listening to what family members are saying. It may convey the attitude that the professional is in charge and will direct what the parent should say. Rather than listening and responding to the parent, the professional may pay too much attention to what question comes next on the checklist or survey.

A final note regarding communication is offered by Winton and Bailey (1990), who emphasize that when opportunities for open discussions are created with families, unexpected or unanticipated concerns and needs may arise. They suggest that developing expertise in interviewing families requires ongoing practice, feedback, and self-assessment.

THE INDIVIDUALIZED FAMILY SERVICE PLAN PROCESS

If the identification of family resources, priorities, and concerns, and subsequent development of outcomes are intended to assist family members in caring for their child with special needs, then the evaluation and assessment of the child should also be a collaborative process involving families and specialists. Kjerland and Kovach (1990) recommend that developmental assessments should:

> take place in a relaxed, collegial atmosphere with staff highly responsive to family priorities, style, and concerns. They occur at a time and location and in a manner that is comfortable and productive for families. Insights for parents and interventionists come from the free interchange of ideas and concerns throughout the entire process, from preparation for assessment to interpretation of findings. (p. 287)

The task, then, is to place families at the center of early intervention services rather than considering them to be an extension of services provided to the child (Kochanek, 1991). Hanson and Freund (1989) discuss four reasons why any model of developmental assessment and intervention should include families at its core. The first is that families function as a system in which events that affect one member affect all members. The second reason acknowledges the role parents play as primary caregivers and the influence they have on their child's development. The third reason recognizes that parents should be the primary decision makers in matters involving their children's programs and related family matters. Finally, parents and professionals have different vantage points when viewing a child's profile of abilities, delays, and priorities for intervention.

Family members need to be included before, during, and after the child's evaluation and assessment. See Appendix A for a list of selected instruments for involving parents in their child's assessment. During first contacts, families and professionals need to introduce one another to their unique perspectives. The early intervention specialists should introduce family members to the program's philosophy and resources, and family members can introduce professionals to their child and inform professionals about their concerns. Negotiating where and when to evaluate and assess the child and how best to interact with the child are decisions in which parents must be involved during the planning component. The actual developmental assessment should be based on exploring the parents' stated concerns at referral, as well as areas identified by early intervention specialists. Kjerland and Kovach (1990) recommend that the assessment begin with a review of its purpose and the procedures chosen by parents and specialists. The pace should be relaxed, following the spontaneous play, movement, and language opportunities presented by the child. Standardized tools and informal observations of the child are both acceptable methods for evaluating and assessing the child.

Following the assessment, parents and professionals have another opportunity to share vital information. Only family members can view the child's performance during the evaluation and assessment as typical or atypical of behavior and abilities in general. Specialists can assist family members in understanding the child from their perspective of having worked with children with similar profiles of abilities and delays. Such discussion leads family members and professionals to a better understanding of the full range and interrelationships of the child's developmental needs and abilities (Kjerland & Kovach, 1990). In turn, the child's developmental profile becomes the central point for identifying what the family already has available to them in the form of supports, resources, and services, what they need to enhance the child's development, how best to provide early intervention services, and how to link the family with other needed services.

Family Assessment: Identifying Family Resources, Priorities, and Concerns

The regulations implementing P. L. 99-457 mandate that family assessment be:

- Designed to identify the "strengths and needs" of the family related to enhancing the development of the child.
- Voluntary on the part of the family, with prior written notice in the family's native language and written parental consent obtained.
- Conducted by personnel trained to utilize appropriate methods and procedures.
- Based on information provided by the family through a personal interview.
- Designed to incorporate the family's description of its strengths and needs related to enhancing the child's development.

Although this provision is referred to as "family assessment," its meaning in early intervention is significantly different from that found in psychotherapy and family therapy literature, which imply an in-depth look at family dynamics, marital relationships, or parent-child interaction (Krauss & Jacobs, 1990). Although such a "family assessment" may be useful for families, it is not the intended outcome of identifying family "strengths and needs" defined in P. L. 99-457.

The phrase "family strengths and needs" has been alternately stated as "family resources, concerns and priorities" to more accurately reflect a family centered philosophy that recognizes the positive attributes of families. "Family strengths," then, are the resources, including people, facilities, and equipment available to the family to help them care for their child. "Family needs" are the family's expressed desires or priorities for anticipated outcomes, early intervention services, and linkage to other needed services.

The purpose of identifying family resources, priorities, and concerns is to assist the family in developing and implementing a service plan that will meet the developmental needs of the child identified during evaluation and assessment. Professionals and families each have critical roles to play in this process. The role of early interventionists is to facilitate families' decision-making concerning outcomes and early intervention services for their children. Family members have the responsibility to facilitate positive relationships with professionals by taking a careful inventory of their family resources and clarifying what services are desired for the child.

Strategies and Methods for Identifying Family Resources, Priorities, and Concerns

The identification of resources, priorities, and concerns must be based on individual preferences, because not all families or family members prefer to share family information or consider their priorities for their children in the same manner (Kaufmann & McGonigel, 1991). According to Bailey (in press),

> Research and common sense suggest that the issue of interviews versus
> surveys is not an either-or question. Rather, the issue is which procedure
> is more useful at a specific time with an individual family and an indi-
> vidual professional for a particular purpose.

Considering the ongoing nature of assessment as it relates to the changing needs of the child and family, Bailey's comment is noteworthy.

Professionals may make specific recommendations to families in the form of options for identifying family resources and priorities. Kaufmann and McGonigel (1991) suggest brainstorming as one way to help families recognize the talents and resources they already have to care for their children and meet their special needs. Other means of addressing this issue include personal interviews and completion of self-report instruments or checklists. See Appendix A for a list of selected instruments. All strategies are dependent on the communication and collaboration skills discussed in the "Foundations for Collaboration" section of this chapter.

Personal Interviews. There are important issues to address with families prior to conducting personal interviews. The primary issue is to explain the purpose of the interview and why it will be helpful to the family and professionals involved in assessing or intervening with the child. It is critical to convey that the purpose is to provide assistance, support, and information to the family rather than to assess their parenting skills or family life. Another issue focuses on how the interview will take place. Rather than defining a set procedure, it is important to ask families where, when, and how they would like to identify family resources, priorities, and concerns. Although programs may not be able to accommodate every family's choice for location and time, family requests for inclusion of specific participants should be honored, if at all possible.

Written Surveys, Checklists, and Questionnaires. Many written measures, both formal and informal, are available to assist families and professionals in this process. Just as participation in family assessment is voluntary, so is the use of written means to identify family resources, priorities, and concerns. If families choose to use them, self-report measures are recommended because they are completed by family members and may be used in a variety of ways. Some families may prefer to fill them in as individual family members or as a group, and review them privately before discussions with professionals. Others may prefer to share completed measures during their personal interview with early intervention specialists.

When selecting written measures and tools for use in identifying family resources, priorities, and concerns, early intervention personnel should assure that instruments:

- Provide the information needed to assist the families served by a particular early intervention program.
- Identify family resources, priorities, and concerns rather than the state of marital relationships or other family dynamics.
- Support cultural diversity and changes in a family's needs and priorities over time.
- Be easily understood in terms of readability and response format.
- Request information in a manner respectful of family privacy.
- Be reliable and valid.

Responses should always be discussed by family members and early intervention specialists involved in the personal interview. This discussion provides an excellent opportunity for professionals to listen to and clarify family messages regarding what they want for their children, and it serves as the link to developing outcomes, identifying early intervention and other services, and documenting decisions.

Developing, Implementing, and Evaluating the IFSP

Developing and Implementing the IFSP

When the child's developmental profile has been determined through evaluation and assessment, and the family has identified related resources, priorities, and concerns, then family members and professionals have an appropriate foundation from which to develop outcomes and recommend services to address identified needs. In an outcome-based process, the identified strengths and needs of the child and the resources and concerns of the family serve as the immediate basis for determining outcomes, as well as for the strategies and activities to achieve them. Family members identify and prioritize changes they would like to see for their child or themselves, with outcomes focusing on any area of child development or family life that a family believes is related to its ability to enhance the child's development (Johnson, McGonigel, & Kaufmann, 1989). Communication of professional perspectives regarding identified outcomes and use of information gathered through open-ended questions, interviews, and surveys can assure that family selected outcomes are based on informed choices.

Selection of appropriate early intervention and linkage services occurs *after* outcomes are developed, when strategies to achieve desired changes result from collaborative discussion of a range of available options that includes already identified family and community resources. Traditionally, professionals have documented a child's strengths and needs through assessment, recommended specific services, and subsequently developed intervention goals and objectives solely on the basis of what the child is unable to do (Campbell, 1990). This approach does not immediately link a service to a goal. In contrast, an outcome-based process explores maximum access to all available system and family resources in the community to meet the identified developmental needs of the child and family and does not automatically link a specific service to a goal.

With outcome decisions reached, families and professionals must meet to document information on a written plan, specifying information as required by federal regulations. The purpose of the initial IFSP meeting is to provide an opportunity to formalize decisions about outcomes and services and to create a tangible framework from which to translate decisions into action. Implementation of the IFSP involves the operationalizing of methods and procedures delineated to meet agreed on outcomes. Figure 1-1 at the end of the chapter, includes one example of a completed IFSP developed by early intervention staff and parents. Other formats have been developed and also may be appropriate for use.

Evaluating the IFSP Process and Document

By defining assessment as "the ongoing procedures used by appropriate personnel throughout the period of a child's eligibility to identify the child's unique needs, the family's strengths and needs related to the development of the child, and the nature and extent of early intervention services that are needed by the child and the child's family," [CFR 34.303.322 (b)(2)] the implementing regulations clearly recognize (1) the dynamic process of infant and toddler development; (2) that change in the child's needs will effect change in the resources, priorities, and concerns of families; and (3) that service strategies may require modification as a result. Thus, the definition itself is the basis for the interrelatedness of the components of the IFSP process.

An effective IFSP process also facilitates ongoing review and revision of outcomes and services for eligible children and their families, beyond the required periodic review cycle of 6 months and annual evaluation. Professionals and families actively engaged in collaborative planning will seek opportunities, both formally and informally, to determine the degree to which outcomes are being achieved and to modify strategies and activities as necessary. Child and family priorities change, either through progress or circumstance, and the IFSP process should provide a workable mechanism to revise the document to reflect current decision-making.

It is essential to request feedback from families when evaluating the overall effectiveness of an early intervention program, as well as outcomes of specific activities and services provided to individual children and families. Deal, Dunst, and Trivette (1989) describe a model for developing flexible IFSPs, which includes a simple rating scale for assessing the effectiveness of staff and family implementation efforts.

SUMMARY

If developing an individualized family service plan is to be anything more than filling in the blank spaces on a document to meet the requirements of federal and state laws, early intervention systems must design processes that are family centered, flexible, and dynamic. Understanding of and commitment to the fundamental concepts of collaboration between families and professionals must be the philosophical premise on which the IFSP process is based. Finally, the process must define component steps in a way that provides a blueprint for systems operation and in a way that recognizes the ongoing and reciprocal relationships of those steps. A cyclical process that provides for continual modification of services to meet family priorities is essential. When identification of child strengths and needs is based on information obtained during first contacts, and identification of family resources, priorities, and concerns is based on the child's developmental profile, then decisions about outcomes and services may be derived from identified needs of the child and family. Conversely, as strategies and activities are implemented and reviewed, changing child and family needs require further identification of resources and priorities, continuing the exchange of information. When families and service providers alike realize that an IFSP is a flexible process rather than a static document, the true potential of early intervention will be achieved.

REFERENCES

Allen, D., & Hudd, S. (1987). Are we professionalizing parents? Weighing the benefits and pitfalls. *American Journal of Mental Retardation, 25*, 133–137.

Anderson, J., & Hinojosa, J. (1984). Parents and therapists in a professional partnership. *American Journal of Occupational Therapy, 38* (7), 452–461.

Bailey, D. (in press). Issues and perspectives on family assessment. *Infants and Young Children.*

Bazyk, S. (1989). Changes in attitude and beliefs regarding parent participation and home programs: An update. *American Journal of Occupational Therapy, 43* (11), 723–730.

Blacher, J. (1982). Sequential stages of parental adjustment to the birth of a child with handicaps: Fact or fiction? *Mental Retardation, 22* (2), 58–68.

Campbell, P. (1990, May). *The individual family service plan: A guide for families and early intervention professionals.* Tallmadge, OH: Family Child Learning Center.

Deal, A., Dunst, C., & Trivette, C. (1989). A flexible and functional approach to developing individualized family service plans. *Infants and Young Children, 1* (4), 32–43.

Duhl, B. (1983). *From the inside out and other metaphors.* New York: Simon & Schuster.

Dunst, C., Trivette, C., & Deal, A. (1988). *Enabling and empowering families: Principles and guidelines for practice.* Cambridge, MA: Brookline Books.

Hanft, B. (Ed.) (1989). *Family-centered care: An early intervention resource manual.* Rockville, MD: American Occupational Therapy Association.

Hanft, B. (1991). Impact of federal policy on pediatric health and education programs. In W. Dunn (Ed.), *Pediatric service delivery* (pp. 273–284). Thorofare, NJ: Slack, Inc.

Hanson, J., & Freund, M. (1989). *A journey with parents and infants: Rethinking parent professional interactions.* Washington, DC: George Washington University.

Hanson, M., Lynch, E., & Wayman, K. (1990). Honoring the cultural diversity of families when gathering data. *Topics in Early Childhood Special Education, 10* (1), 112–131.

Johnston, M. (1980). Cultural variations in professional and parenting patterns. *Journal of Gynecological and Neonatal Nursing*, *9* (1), 9–13.

Johnson, B., McGonigel, M., & Kaufmann, R. (Eds.) (1989). *Guidelines and recommended practices for the individualized family service plan*. Chapel Hill, NC and Bethesda, MD: NEC∗TAS and Association for the Care of Children's Health.

Kaufmann, R., & McGonigel, M. (1991). Identifying family concerns, priorities, and resources. In M. McGonigel, R. Kaufmann, & B. Johnson (Eds.), *Guidelines and recommended practices for the individualized family service plan* (2nd ed.) (pp. 47–55). Bethesda, MD: Association for the Care of Children's Health.

Kjerland, L., & Kovach, J. (1990). Family-staff collaboration for tailored infant assessment. In E. Gibbs & D. Teti (Eds.), Interdisciplinary assessment of infants (pp. 287–298). Baltimore, MD: Paul H. Brookes.

Kochanek, T. (1991). Translating family policy into early intervention initiatives: Preliminary outcomes and implications. *Infants and Young Children*, *3* (4), 12–37.

Krauss, M., & Jacobs, F. (1990). Family assessment: Purposes and techniques. In S. Meisels & J. Shonkoff (Eds.), *Handbook of early childhood intervention* (pp. 303–325). New York: Cambridge University Press.

Lipsky, D. (1985). A parental perspective on stress and coping. *American Journal of Orthopsychiatry*, *55* (4), 614–617.

Mead, M. (1956). Understanding cultural diversity. *Nursing Outlook*, *4* (5), 260–262.

Miller, L., Lynch, E., & Campbell, J. (1990). Parents as partners: A new paradigm for collaboration. *Best Practices in School Speech-Language Pathology*, *1*, 40–56.

Murphy, M. (1982). The family with a handicapped child. *Developmental Behavioral Pediatrics Journal*, *2* (3), 73–81.

Pizzo, P. (1983). *Parent to parent: Working together for ourselves and our children*. Boston: Beacon Press.

Pizzo, P. (1990). Parent advocacy: A resource for early intervention. In S. Meisels & J. Shonkoff (Eds.), *Handbook of early childhood intervention* (pp. 668–678). New York: Cambridge University Press.

Powell, D. (1988). Emerging directions in parent-child early intervention. In D. Powell (Ed.), *Parent education as early childhood intervention: Emerging directions in theory, research, and practice* (pp. 1–22). Norwood, NJ: Ablex.

Satir, V. (1972). *People making*. Palo Alto, CA: Science and Behavior Books.

Seitz, V., & Provence, S. (1990). Caregiver-focused models of early intervention. In S. Meisels & J. Shonkoff (Eds.), *Handbook of early childhood intervention* (pp. 400–427). New York: Cambridge University Press.

Shelton, T., Jeppson, E., & Johnson, B. (Eds.). (1987). *Family centered care for children with special health care needs*. Washington, DC: Association for the Care of Children's Health.

Smolak, L. (1986). *Infancy*. Englewood Cliffs, NJ: Prentice-Hall.

Summers, J., Dell'Oliver, C., Turnbull, A., Benson, H., Santelli, E., Campbell, M., & Siegel-Causey, E. (in press). Focusing in on the IFSP process: What are family differences? *Topics in Early Childhood Special Education*.

Travis, G. (1976). *Chronic illness in children: Its impact on child and family*. Stanford, CA: Stanford University Press.

Versluys, H. (1980). Rehabilitation and family dynamics. *Rehabilitation Literature*, *3-4* (41), 58–65.

Vincent, L., Salisbury, C., Strain, P., McCormick, C., & Tessier, A. (1990). A behavioral-ecological approach to early intervention: Focus on cultural diversity. In S. Meisels & J. Shonkoff (Eds.), *Handbook of early intervention* (pp. 173–195). New York: Cambridge University Press.

Winton, P., & Bailey, D. (1990). Early intervention training related to family interviewing. *Topics in Early Childhood Special Education*, *10* (1), 50–62.

Figure 1-1
Individualized Family Service Plan (IFSP)

INDIVIDUALIZED FAMILY SERVICE PLAN (IFSP)

Child's Name: _Bruce C. Baxter_   **Phone:** _433-9760_   **Address:** _1416 E. Belvedere Avenue_
     Baltimore, MD 21239

Child's Birthdate: _8-15-88_

Parent(s) Name(s): _Bonnie M & Clyde F._   **Phone:** _433-9760_   **Address:** _Same as above_

Case Manager's Name: _Glenda Johns_   **Phone:** _433-9236_   **Agency/Address:** _Baltimore City Public Schools_
     200 E. North Avenue
     Baltimore, MD 21202

REFERRAL DATE: _11-19-88_

MEETING DATE: _1-2-89_

IFSP TYPE:
____ Interim
_✓_ Initial
____ Annual Evaluation

TRANSITION PLAN ATTACHED: ____ Yes   _✓_ Not Applicable

PART I: IFSP TEAM

Parent(s)/Family:
I [We] have had the opportunity to participate in the development of this IFSP. I [We] have been informed of my [our] rights under this program, through receipt of the Early Intervention System Parents' Rights Brochure. I [We] understand the plan, and parental rights, and **I [we] give permission** to implement this plan.

Bonnie M. Baxter   _Clyde F. Baxter_   _1/2/89_
Signature of Parent(s)/Guardian/Surrogate   Date

Other IFSP Meeting Participants:
Each agency or person who has a direct role in the provision of early intervention services is responsible for making a good faith effort to assist each eligible child and their family in achieving the outcomes on the child's IFSP.

Glenda Johns, OTR   _BCPS_   _Jeff Ramsay, LPT_   _BCPS_
Signature/Interim Case Manager   Agency & Title   Signature   Agency & Title

Same as above   _Elise Jenkins, R.S._   _BCHD_
Signature/Case Manager   Agency & Title   Signature   Agency & Title

Lydia Von Vorhouse, Program Director
Signature/Lead Agency Representative   Agency & Title   Signature   Agency & Title

_____   _____
Signature   Agency & Title   Signature   Agency & Title

17

PART II: CHILD'S DEVELOPMENTAL STATUS AND FAMILY INFORMATION

A. CHILD'S PRESENT LEVELS OF DEVELOPMENT

Area	Date of Procedure	Chron. Age	Age Level/Age Range
Cognitive	12-7-88	4 mos.	1-3 mos.
Speech/Language	"	"	0-3 mos.
Psychosocial	"	"	1-3 mos.
Self-help	"	"	0-2 mos.
Health Status:	Dr. Rose Wink (Primary Health Care Provider)		

Bruce born prematurely at 34 wks gestation, was placed + in a NICU at birth. He was on oxygen therapy for several days and was fed through an NG tube. General health status is now good & Bruce has been released to the care of a local pediatrician. He continues on an apnea monitor at home.

Area	Date of Procedure	Chron. Age	Age Level/Age Range
Physical:			
Fine Motor	12-7-88	4 mos.	0-2 mos.
Gross Motor	"	"	0-2 mos.
Hearing	11-29-88	3 mos.	WNL
Vision	11-29-88	3 mos.	

+ Vision screening was inconclusive, but due to oxygen therapy, Bruce should be rechecked.

+ indicates space for recording status of child's hearing, vision, and health

B. CHILD'S STRENGTHS AND NEEDS

Strengths: Bruce's general health is now stable and he is awake and alert for increasing periods of time. He responds to familiar voices, likes to be held, and is beginning to show interest in toys placed in his hands.

Needs: Bruce needs to develop a better sucking & swallowing pattern. He also needs to improve motor skills so he can play with his toys & explore them. Bruce needs to have his vision rechecked because decisions about ways to work with him should be based on how well he can see. Finally, Bruce is easily distracted & Bonnie wants to participate in planned sessions so any home based direct services may need to be scheduled at x-home when Mrs 3 year old Betsy is at preschool or being watched by a neighbor.

C. FAMILY STRENGTHS AND NEEDS RELATED TO ENHANCING THE CHILD'S DEVELOPMENT (voluntary on part of family)

Strengths: Bonnie is not working outside the home, so has time to be at home with Bruce. She has some training in child development, has a preschooler, and has cared for other infants, although none with special needs. Bonnie & Clyde have nearby relatives & friends who have volunteered to help in any way they can, including caring for either child who otherwise may. Another identified support is the local pediatrician, Dr. Roy Wink, who monitors Bruce & advises the Setters re: use of the apnea monitor.

Needs: Bonnie & Clyde would like to:
1) learn more about Bruce's needs
2) Meet other parents of children with similar needs
3) Find a program that teaches infant CPR in order to accept child care offers from friends & relatives
4) Schedule Bruce's therapy sessions at times when out-of-home arrangements can be made for Bruce's sister, Betsy.

PART III: CHILD/FAMILY OUTCOMES RELATED TO CHILD DEVELOPMENT (Related to eligible services under Part H)

Outcome # 1 _Improved motor development and feeding skills for Bruce._

Strategies/Activities: Glenda & Joy will coordinate occupational and physical therapies for Bruce in order to support each other's activities. To do so, they will see him together one weekly for a month, then see him individually once each week. Activities will enable Bruce to:
(a) develop a smooth, coordinated suck & swallow
(b) sit erect, supported, with head at mid-line and chin tucked during feeding
(c) increase hand-to-mouth play
(d) manipulate a toy using both hands at mid-line

Criteria/Timelines: Glenda & Joy will monitor Bruce's progress by observations during feedings & interactive play. Formal reassessment will be conducted in three months.

Person(s) Responsible: Glenda Johns, OTR
(Name, Title, Phone #)   433-9236
                                        Joy Ramsey, PT &
Bonnie & Clyde Barker, Parents
Ending Date:

Outcome # 2 _An appropriate diet for Bruce, based on nutritional counseling_

Strategies/Activities: Elsie will meet with Bonnie and/or Clyde at the Health Dept. to review Bruce's status regarding amount and manner of food intake. Based on parent report and current medical information, Elsie will recommend necessary changes in caloric intake, dietary supplements, as well as variety and texture of foods, when appropriate.

Elsie will speak with Bruce's pediatrician by telephone on a monthly basis to obtain necessary medical information.

Criteria/Timelines: An appt. will be scheduled 1X monthly, at least until the 6 mo. review. Elsie will monitor Bruce's nutritional progress through parent report and by checking medical reports of her & Joy's guide & general health status.

Person(s) Responsible:
(Name, Title, Phone #)
Elsie Jenkins, R.D. / _Bonnie & Clyde, Barker, Parents_

Ending Date:

Outcome #3 _Evaluation of Bruce's vision_

Strategies/Activities: Visual acuity evaluation will be scheduled through the Opthamology Clinic at the University of Maryland Hospital. If Bonnie needs a ride to the clinic because Clyde can't take time off from work, a neighbor has offered to drive.

Criteria/Timelines: Glenda will assist the Barkers to schedule an appt. for Bruce between now & March 1994. At the latest, an updated report regarding Bruce's vision status will be available by the 6 month review of the ISP.

Person(s) Responsible: Glenda Johns, OTR, Con
(Name, Title, Phone #)   (schedule)
Jason Marigold, M.D. (evaluate)
Ending Date:

PART IV: EARLY INTERVENTION PROGRAM SERVICES (Eligible services under Part H)

Service: _Occupational Therapy_

Provider Name: _Glenda Johns, OTR_

Provider Agency: _Baltimore City Public Schools_

Frequency: _1X weekly_   Intensity: _45 min._   Basis: __ Group   ✓Individual

Location: _Home_   Financial Responsibility: _Local Education Agency_

Initiation Date: _1/9/89_   Projected Duration: _7/89_

Addition Date: ____
Modification Date: ____
Ending Date: ____

Service: _Physical Therapy_

Provider Name: _Joy Ramsey, LPT_

Provider Agency: _Baltimore City Public Schools_

Frequency: _1X weekly_   Intensity: _45 min._   Basis: __ Group   ✓Individual

Location: _Home_   Financial Responsibility: _Purchase of Service – Education_

Initiation Date: _1/9/89_   Projected Duration: _7/89_

Addition Date: ____
Modification Date: ____
Ending Date: ____

Service: _Nutrition_

Provider Name: _Elsie Jenkins, R.D._

Provider Agency: _Baltimore City Health Department_

Frequency: _1x monthly_   Intensity: _30 min._   Basis: __ Group   ✓Individual

Location: _Other setting (Health Department)_   Financial Responsibility: _Local Health Department_

Initiation Date: _1/12/89_   Projected Duration: _7/89_

Addition Date: ____
Modification Date: ____
Ending Date: ____

PART IV: EARLY INTERVENTION PROGRAM SERVICES (Eligible services under Part H)

Service: _Assessment (Ophthalmologic Evaluation)_

Provider Name: _Jason Marigold, M.D._

Provider Agency: _University of MD Hospital_

Frequency: _1x only_   **Intensity:** _60 min._   **Basis:** ___ Group   _✓_ Individual

Location: _Outpatient Service Facility_   **Financial Responsibility:** _Medical Assistance (MA7507)_

Initiation Date: _1/3/89_   **Projected Duration:** _3/89_

Addition Date: ___
Modification Date: ___
Ending Date: ___

Service: ___

Provider Name: ___

Provider Agency: ___

Frequency: ___   **Intensity:** ___   **Basis:** ___ Group ___ Individual

Location: ___   **Financial Responsibility:** ___

Initiation Date: ___   **Projected Duration:** ___

Addition Date: ___
Modification Date: ___
Ending Date: ___

Service: ___

Provider Name: ___

Provider Agency: ___

Frequency: ___   **Intensity:** ___   **Basis:** ___ Group ___ Individual

Location: ___   **Financial Responsibility:** ___

Initiation Date: ___   **Projected Duration:** ___

Addition Date: ___
Modification Date: ___
Ending Date: ___

21

Child's Name: _Bruce C. Carter_

PART V: OTHER CHILD/FAMILY OUTCOMES (Related to non-required services under Part H)

Outcome #1 Infant CPR training for two relatives so they may care for Bruce in Bonnie & Clyde's absence.

Strategies/Activities:
Glenda will help Bonnie & Clyde identify community programs that teach infant CPR at no cost.

Possibilities: Red Cross
YMCA
Local hospital
Family Support Center

Criteria/Timelines: List of available no cost infant CPR training programs in the community will be given to Bonnie & Clyde by the end of January, 1989, so they can

Person(s) Responsible: Glenda Johns, OTR, CM
(Name, Title, Phone #) 433-9236
Bonnie & Clyde Carter, Parents
Ending Date:

Outcome #2 Bonnie & Clyde would like Betsy to attend a preschool program, at least on the days Bruce is scheduled for therapy.

Strategies/Activities:
Glenda will help Bonnie & Clyde identify community preschool programs that accept children of Betsy's age.

A neighbor has agreed to provide transportation for Betsy on the mornings she attends preschool, so Bonnie does not have to reschedule Bruce's therapy time.

Criteria/Timelines: By mid-January, 1989, a list of community preschool programs will be given to Bonnie & Clyde, so they can initiate contacts and arrange enrollment.

Person(s) Responsible: Glenda Johns, OTR, CM
(Name, Title, Phone #) 433-9236
Bonnie & Clyde Carter, Parents
Ending Date:

Outcome #

Strategies/Activities:

Criteria/Timelines:

Person(s) Responsible:
(Name, Title, Phone #)

Ending Date:

Child's Name: *Bruce C. Carter*

PART VI: SERVICE LINKAGES FOR OTHER CHILD/FAMILY OUTCOMES (Non-required services under Part H)

Service: *Other (CPR training)*

Provider Agency:

Funding Source(s): *No Fee*

Primary Client: *Other relative*

Addition Date:
Modification Date:
Ending Date:

Service: *Preschool Program*

Provider Agency:

Funding Source(s): *Sliding fees - Parent Payment*

Primary Client: *Sibling*

Addition Date:
Modification Date:
Ending Date:

Service:

Provider Agency:

Funding Source(s):

Primary Client:

Addition Date:
Modification Date:
Ending Date:

Service:

Provider Agency:

Funding Source(s):

Primary Client:

Addition Date:
Modification Date:
Ending Date:

Service:

Provider Agency:

Funding Source(s):

Primary Client:

Addition Date:
Modification Date:
Ending Date:

Service:

Provider Agency:

Funding Source(s):

Primary Client:

Addition Date:
Modification Date:
Ending Date:

Service:

Provider Agency:

Funding Source(s):

Primary Client:

Addition Date:
Modification Date:
Ending Date:

PART VII: TRANSITION PLAN

Transition Plan Provisions	Date Initiated	Date Completed
Discuss community program options for child	_____	_____
Discuss community program options for family	_____	_____
Provide parental rights and responsibilities (i.e., procedural safeguards)	_____	_____
Identify, schedule, and conduct evaluations/assessments/procedures to determine eligibility for programs	_____	_____
Identify program options for child based on results of evaluations/assessments/procedures	_____	_____
Identify and implement steps to assist families in evaluating available and eligible programs and services	_____	_____
Identify and implement steps to assist families in accessing available and eligible programs and services	_____	_____
Transmit specified information to local education agency, with written consent from parents (when child will receive special education and related services - Part B)	_____	_____
Transmit specified information to other community programs, upon parent request	_____	_____
Identify and implement steps to help child adjust to and function in new environments	_____	_____

TRANSITION TO:

_Part B Services

Child Care/Enrichment
_In-home Child Care
_School-age Child Care
_Preschool Program
_Head Start
_Camps, Day/Residential
_Tutoring

Medical/Health
_Diagnostic/Advisory Clinics
_Equipment/Devices
_Home Health Care
_Hospitalization
_Immunizations
_Mental Health Services
_Primary Health Care
_Surgical Procedure
_WIC Program

Other
_Parent Education
_Support Group
_Recreation Program
_Other (specify)
_____
_____
_____
_____

Chapter 2

Mental Health Needs of Infants and Their Families

NANCY DONOHUE COLLETTA

Adults have a vested interest in believing that the very young are protected from the worst things in life. Even when there is evidence that infants are damaged at birth or soon after, one likes to believe that their emotional well being is resilient and protected by the adults around them. However, to provide comprehensive services for infants and their families, a harsher reality must be faced; emotional development and mental health are seriously vulnerable to damage in the first three years of life.

This chapter focuses on the incidence and identification of mental health problems in infancy. The first question asked is, What signs do we see that indicate an infant has a mental health problem? The chapter then reviews information on groups of infants who are at risk for developing problems: temperamentally difficult infants, drug-exposed infants, abused and neglected infants, and infants whose parents have severe social and emotional problems. Once aware of the scope and description of the problems, methods of working with families and caregivers to improve infant mental health are considered.

ASSUMPTIONS

As a foundation for discussion, it is important to make some general assumptions about the emotional development of infants and toddlers. These assumptions are based on studies (Schaffer, 1990) that are relevant to both planning programs and working with infants and their families.

1. *At the most basic level, infant emotional problems may be thought of as originating in the match between the needs of the infant and the family's resources.* Most times there is an adequate match, with the infant not having excessive needs, and the family having enough resources to meet those needs on at least a basic level. If there is an imbalance, the needs of the infant are too high, or the resources of the family are depleted, there is likely to be a negative impact on the infant's emotional development.

2. *Long-term negative circumstances rather than single events have the greatest impact on children's mental health.* It is clear that single events when compared to chronic problems are much less likely to mark the child for life. For example, although professionals worry about events such as separating infants and preschoolers from their parents, research has revealed that it is seldom a single event such as separation that causes long-term problems for children. Rather it is the long-lasting circumstances, such as conflicts and tensions leading up to and following a separation, that determine the extent and duration of emotional distress.

3. *Children's emotional well-being is most adversely affected when multiple stresses build up in their lives.* Determining which children are at highest risk for mental health problems means professionals need to take into account the interaction of multiple risk factors. For example, it is known that premature babies are at risk for a host of later complications. However, because the majority of premature babies develop few, if any problems, it would be poor use of resources to offer services to all premature babies. Rather, professionals need to consider multiple risks: birth factors; poverty; parental social and emotional functioning; and child characteristics such as sex, birth order, and temperament when placing a child in an "at risk" group for services.

4. *Children's emotions develop as part of a unified system; when one area of development is adversely affected, other areas of development are at risk as well.* When a child is damaged in one area, it is important to evaluate all areas of development for evidence of delays. For example, if a child's emotional well-being is seriously impaired, cognitive and language development are likely to suffer. This is in part because a damaged emotional, physical, or developmental area often becomes the focus of the child's attention, preoccupying the child and draining him or her of the energy to devote to other developmental tasks.

5. *The longer negative circumstances are allowed to continue in a child's life, the more difficult they become to change.* Children who suffer serious early trauma, neglect, abuse, or deprivation, but who are removed to more favorable environments are in fact able to recuperate. However, it is important to recognize that if interventions are not made, the negative impact builds up, with the effects being subtle in infants, and becoming more pronounced as the child enters the preschool and school years. For example, aggressive, hostile, and acting-out behavior problems when seen in the preschool years, do not readily go away by themselves and in fact become worse without intervention.

IDENTIFYING INFANT MENTAL HEALTH PROBLEMS

Much of the clinical work done with babies does not start out with a known problem or a definite diagnosis because babies cannot directly describe their distress. Babies do, however, use the bodily functions and the communication abilities they have to give clues to their emotional reactions. Thus, the youngest infants show their distress in poorly regulated bodily functions and difficulties in relating to people; older infants also use developing motor skills to signal distress, and in the preschool years words and more complicated behaviors come into play to express problems. As an example, consider the baby who has difficulties with an overly intrusive and controlling mother. As the baby develops each new skill area the struggle is played out; at 4 months when the baby has control over only his head, neck, and eyes, the baby looks away from the intrusive mother; at 7 months the baby uses gestures to say "no!"; at 14 months the baby is able to run from his mother; and by 2 years the baby begins to use language in his struggle with the mother (Stern, 1985).

Infants and young children give us signals that tell something is wrong. Signals are used when the child does not yet have words to tell his or her parents how he or she feels or when the older child finds it easier to get parental attention through behavior rather than through words. The signals of children's emotional distress may be hard to recognize for what they are, but they almost always make parents anxious or angry. Parents often view these signals as the child's attempt to make their lives difficult, rather than as an attempt to communicate a need. Infants and children quickly learn which of their behaviors push their parent's buttons, hit a sensitive spot, and thus increase the likelihood that they will receive the attention they need.

A major issue in infant mental health work is differentiating between *normal difficulties* and *signals of serious problems*. Most young children and their parents have some difficulty adjusting to developmental transitions and expectable upsets. There may be sleep disturbances after a change in caregivers, a period when tantrums are the daily routine, or a time of intense fear of being away from the mother. In general, the normal is separated from the abnormal in terms of duration and intensity of the child's behavior. Although there is no absolute standard, a child's emotional reactions and mental health are of concern when the behavior:

- Is far more intense than expected for a child of the same age
- Lasts for longer than 6 weeks
- Disturbs the child's ability to function in other developmental areas
- Causes serious distress to the family.

It is also important to note that behaviors have different meanings depending on the age of the child and the circumstances surrounding the behavior. Bed wetting is acceptable in a 2 year old who is just being toilet trained, a probable regression in a 4 year old with an infant sibling, and more serious in a 6 year old whose parents are in intense conflict.

There are characteristic ways in which mental health problems show up in infant behavior and development. Although the following signals may be an indication of emotional distress, physical and developmental causes always should be investigated. Emotional distress in the first three years of life may be seen in

(a) *patterns of social contact:*

1. The baby may be withdrawn from interacting with people, may make poor eye contact, show a lack of interest in people, or not differentiate between familiar and unfamiliar adults.
2. The baby may be highly ambivalent in interactions with caregivers, sometimes clinging, sometimes pushing them away in anger.
3. The baby may show an inability to regulate his or her responses to social interaction to the point that he or she becomes overexcited and unable to soothe him- or herself after relatively small amounts of interaction.

(b) *poor regulation of bodily functions:*

1. The baby may have problems with eating; eating an abnormally large or small amount of food, having frequent gas or stomach upsets, or vomiting food.
2. The baby may show a sleep disturbance; difficulty falling asleep, frequent waking during the night, waking very early in the morning without being able to go back to sleep, or sleeping abnormally long periods of time.
3. The baby may have difficulties with elimination; frequent loose stools or constipation, difficulties with toilet training, bed wetting, or wetting and soiling after training has been completed.

(c) *the infant's emotional expression:*

1. The baby may show signs of depression; it is now recognized that infants may suffer from depression with sadness of face, decreased energy, loss of appetite, and inconsolable crying. In older preschoolers, depression often takes the form of a quiet sadness, withdrawal, becoming too quickly and intensely aggressive, irritable behavior, and shame over some real or imagined deficit.

2. The baby may be angry and hostile; crying in rage, striking out at people or objects, or stiffening the body against physical contact.

3. The baby may show an absence of emotional expressiveness, fleeting eye contact or a blank stare; or show no display of joy, pleasure, anger or fear.

(d) *delays in language and cognitive skills:*

1. Delays in language and cognitive development may be of organic, environmental, or emotional origin. When children are preoccupied by emotional problems they often do not have enough remaining energy to invest in other areas of development. When interactions with caregivers are seriously inappropriate, inconsistent, or illogical, the baby often fails to receive sufficient reinforcement for his attempts at communication, and his language development is seriously hampered.

(e) *aggression turned against the self:*

1. The baby or young child may pull his own hair, bite himself, bang his head, or have a series of "accidents" to communicate his emotional distress.

(f) *aggression turned against other people:*

1. The baby or young child may be highly defiant to adult directives, unable to control his or her impulses, striking out at others by hitting, biting, or kicking.

INFANTS AT HIGH RISK FOR DIFFICULTIES IN EMOTIONAL DEVELOPMENT

Temperamentally Difficult Infants

Difficult temperaments can make babies so hard to care for that their unusual needs threaten to overwhelm even the most competent caregiver. These infants are often at high risk for mental health problems. They may display a variety of characteristics. They may have extremely negative reactions to new situations, show low social interest and withdraw in the face of stress, have highly irregular patterns of eating and sleeping, or have violent tantrums when overloaded by the number of things happening around them. In contrast, temperamentally easy children are highly interested in the social world, have a generally positive mood, adapt well to new people and situations, and have regular patterns of eating and sleeping. Temperamental characteristics are biologically based, may be observed in the first days after birth, and exert an influence throughout life. Parents and caregivers can influence how a child's temperament is expressed, but they also are greatly influenced by it.

Temperamental traits fall on a continuum from very easy to very difficult, (Chess & Thomas 1987). For example, a child who is low on adaptability will fight any change in routine; the infant will refuse a new food, the toddler will not want to go to the playground and then will not want to leave, and the preschooler will have difficulty adjusting to new caregivers or to school. The child with little social interest will not make easy eye contact as a newborn, will seldom enjoy social play, and will withdraw in the face of too much social interaction. According to Chess and Thomas (1987), the most commonly described temperamental characteristics are:

1. *Activity level*: Level of activity may range from active and restless to quiet and passive.
2. *Mood*: The child may show a basically positive or negative mood or one that varies with the situation.
3. *Adaptability*: The child may find it easy to cope with changes or may have intense reactions to changes.
4. *Approach/withdrawal*: The child may enjoy new people, places and events, or may withdraw from anything that appears new or strange.
5. *Sensory threshold*: Children vary in how easily they are bothered by noise, things to look at, the feel of clothes, or smells.
6. *Persistence*: The child may be extremely persistent when working on a task or may be easily distracted by sights, sounds, or social interaction.
7. *Intensity*: The child may react mildly or with an extreme loudness and intensity.
8. *Distractibility*: The child may be able to pay attention for relatively long periods of time or he may be easily distracted.
9. *Regularity*: The child's sleeping, eating, and eliminating may fall into a predictable pattern or may be highly irregular.
10. *Social interest*: The child may be more interested in objects than in people, may find eye contact uncomfortable, and engage only briefly in social interaction. The highly social child may work to maintain adult attention through social interaction, spend long periods in social play, and spend an unusual amount of energy on developing language skills.

An estimated 10 to 20% of children fall into a temperamentally difficult group (Turecki, 1985). These children are not spoiled or poorly raised, rather there is a definite and difficult pattern in the way they react to the world. The difficult child often generates feelings of confusion, anger, guilt, and exhaustion in the parents. The child and the parent frequently engage in tremendous power struggles, ineffective discipline stems from parental fear of the child's intense reactions, and parental anger may lead to verbal and physical abuse.

Turecki (1985) points out that the difficult child is likely to develop secondary problems in reaction to a negative cycle of interaction with his parents. These secondary problems consist of low self-esteem, anger, fear, and poorly controlled behavior. Very young children with difficult temperaments, most notably inflexibility in response to changes in the environment, high energy level and low adaptability to others' demands, tend to have more behavioral problems and poorer emotional adjustment (Barron & Earls, 1984). Problems are greatest for children when there is a combination of negative factors; for example, difficult temperament combined with high family stress and poor parenting.

Raising a temperamentally difficult child is demanding enough for any well functioning mother or father with few other life stresses. When the parent is single, isolated, with mental health problems, or stressed by poverty, circumstances can deteriorate readily. Consider a teenage mother with a temperamentally difficult preschooler who is active and impulsive, with unpredictable mood changes and intense reactions to new situations. It would not be unlikely that this mother would feel unable to take her child out in public, be criticized by her family for poor parenting, be exhausted by her "human tornado," angry about the limitations the child is putting on her life, and convinced that the child is "doing it on purpose."

Turecki (1985) provides descriptions of what temperamentally difficult traits look like in infancy. These traits include:

1. *High activity level*: The highly active baby may have moved a lot in utero. As an infant the baby is restless in sleep, frequently kicking blankets off. The baby wiggles so much he is hard to bathe and change and has to be watched so accidents do not happen.
2. *High intensity*: The baby screams, cries with unusual intensity and shrieks with delight.
3. *Irregular*: The irregular baby has unpredictable feeding and sleeping schedules.
4. *Low sensory threshold*: The baby is easily overstimulated, reacting strongly to light, noise, being touched, to the feel of clothing, or to the taste of foods.
5. *Initial withdrawal*: The baby complains, cries, or withdraws when faced with new foods, new experiences or new people.
6. *Poor adaptability*: The baby does not like changes in routine or schedule. The baby takes a long time to warm up to new situations or people, and fusses or cries for long periods of time.

7. *Negative mood*: The baby is often cranky, whimpering and crying frequently.

It is important to add the introverted or socially withdrawn baby to this list. The introverted baby is a baby who does not make eye contact, or is comfortable with only brief eye contact, who would rather look at things than at people, and looks away, yawns, or goes to sleep to avoid prolonged interaction. This sort of introversion exerts a powerful influence on the amount of affection and stimulation a baby receives. Consider two depressed mothers, one with an extroverted baby and one with an introverted baby. The extroverted or socially interested baby looks his mother in the eye, smiles, coos, and wiggles in excitement, exerting mighty effort to pulling his mother into social interactions. The introverted baby on the other hand, needs someone to pull him into social interactions. If left to their own devices, the depressed mother and introverted baby withdraw to their own worlds, the baby left alone in his crib, the mother with her gloomy thoughts.

What Interventions Are Needed by the Temperamentally Difficult Child?

Even with a child who appears to have a difficult temperament, it is necessary to eliminate other possible problems before deciding that temperament is the main issue. Physical difficulties such as feeding problems, allergies, or developmental delays should always be investigated and ruled out. If it is determined that the child's temperament is a problem, there are three major ways of intervening to increase the match between the child and the environment (Williamson & Zeitlin, in press):

- Change your demands to be closer to what the child can do.
- Change what the child is able to do by teaching new skills.
- Change your responses to the child.

Examples of these options are detailed in the following paragraphs.

1. *Begin to establish a schedule for the unpredictable baby*. An irregular baby will have no predictable sleeping, eating, or eliminating schedule. Because unpredictable sleeping patterns are most disruptive for families, they need to be regularized first. The baby's schedule might be as follows: One night the baby might sleep for 10 hours, followed by a second night of two 1 hour sleeping periods, and a third night when the baby wants to be up all night and sleep all day. Following this schedule would lead to exhausted parents and a chaotic family life. On the other hand, trying to put the baby on a rigid 7 P.M. to 7 A.M. schedule would be futile and result in frustrated parents and a screaming baby. Ferber, in

Solve Your Child's Sleep Problems (1985) makes excellent suggestions for a baby who has difficulties with sleeping. For example, parents may wake the baby at a consistent time each morning and shorten the baby's daytime naps so that he or she will be more tired at night and make nighttime waking as quiet and uneventful as possible (no lights, talking, or playing with the baby).

2. *Reduce the stimulation for the baby with the low sensory threshold*. Determine what the baby is reacting to. Babies may be sensitive to:

- Sights; bright colors, an abundance of things to look at, things that have too many details
- Social interaction; becomes exhausted, overwhelmed, or has tantrums with much interaction with people, in shopping centers, church, restaurants
- Sounds; with extreme startle in response to noise, wakes up at the slightest sound, is distracted from play by noises
- Textures and temperatures; is irritated by certain clothing, wet diapers, and hot and cold
- Taste; may reject many foods.

Once it is clear what the baby is reacting to, it is possible to make modifications to reduce distress; clothes can be chosen for the child who is hypersensitive to texture to eliminate the morning getting dressed battle; temperatures of bottles and food can be experimented with for the baby who is sensitive to hot and cold; the amount of social interaction can be monitored for the child who is regularly overwhelmed in crowded settings.

3. *Introduce changes gradually for the baby with poor adaptability*. For this type of child routines and predictability are the keys to family peace. New experiences need to be introduced gradually and from a safe distance. This tactic means that new people, things, and experiences are kept at a distance, and the child is gradually allowed to become familiar with them. The child also needs to know the steps or sequence of what will happen and have a warning time before a change actually has to be made.

4. *Set clear limits for the high intensity or negative mood baby*. Often the temperamentally difficult child is so hard to manage that parents feel frustrated, angry, and persecuted by the child, leading them to react emotionally and not use good disciplinary techniques. Parents first must be able to step back long enough to control their own emotions and assess what the child needs. It is also important that the parent be able to differentiate between a temperamental response, when the child cannot seem to help how he or she is responding, and willful manipulation, when the

child is attempting to get his or her own way. The distinction can be understood in the difference between the tantrum of the child who has "overloaded" after a day of shopping and the tantrum of the child whose mother has just said no to more sweets.

Principles of good discipline that are useful with most children are crucial in managing the behavior of the temperamentally difficult child. The following suggestions are good disciplinary practices that should be emphasized with the temperamentally difficult child:

- Make sure the child knows what behavior is expected of him or her.
- Get the child's attention before giving directions.
- Only give directions that you are willing to enforce immediately (If you don't mean it, don't say it).
- Intervene early before behavior gets out of hand.
- Follow noncompliance with immediate action.
- Do not give second or third chances; do not warn or negotiate.

Drug-Exposed Infants

Another group of infants who are at high risk for developing emotional and behavioral problems are those who were prenatally exposed to drugs. Estimates of the numbers of newborns who are prenatally exposed vary from 2 to 11% (Besharov, 1990). Rates vary depending on what is included in the survey; the higher rates include all illegal drugs (rather than just cocaine), with samples coming from large metropolitan areas. Lower rates often refer to single drug use and include samples from more rural areas.

Drug use coexists with a host of other problems. For example, drug-abusing mothers tend to be in their twenties and thirties and usually have two to four other children (Department of Health and Human Services, 1990). Drug abuse often coexists with:

- Poor maternal health
- Inadequate nutrition
- Poor prenatal care
- Intergenerational family dysfunction
- Poly drug use (combinations of cocaine, smoking, drinking, marijuana)
- Other serious psychiatric impairments in the mother, for example, borderline personality disorder, bipolar depression, moderate to severe depression
- AIDS; fully 80% of pediatric AIDS cases are the result of drug abuse by the mother or her sexual partner (Department of Health and Human Services, 1990)

- Family violence; one third of pregnant drug-dependent women report being beaten as children; three quarters report being beaten as adults (Finnegan, 1982).

Contrary to common belief, knowledge of the effects of drugs does not stop the abuse. Interviews with crack-addicted mothers have shown that the majority knew the effect of crack on their unborn children. This knowledge led them to use more crack in an effort to avoid feeling remorse and self-loathing (Chavkin & Kandall, 1990).

Drug-exposed children also are at high risk for abuse. Cocaine, for example, is a "mean drug" that induces high levels of parental violence and neglect. Parents become so preoccupied with feeding their habit that they neglect to feed their children (Besharov, 1990); "Parents who are addicted to drugs have a primary commitment to chemicals, not to their children" (Howard, Beckwith, Rodning & Kropenske, 1989, p. 8).

Drug-exposed newborns most often show patterns of what appears to be damage to their central nervous system. There is no typical profile of the drug-exposed newborn, because damage varies by number, amounts, types of drugs used, and the time during the pregnancy when the drugs were used. For example, if cocaine is used in the first trimester, the child suffers intrauterine growth retardation, and is born small for gestational age. If cocaine use continues, more immediate and direct effects are seen, such as the baby being jittery and overexcited. It is beginning to appear that prenatal damage is severely exacerbated by a chaotic or understimulating early environment.

Problems in the drug-exposed infant may be extreme hydrocephaly, poor brain growth, kidney problems, and sudden infant death syndrome. Drug-exposed babies also are likely to be premature, hypersensitive, irritable, with inconsolable high-pitched screaming, and a disordered sleep-wake cycle. Sleep cycles may be as short as 45 minutes day and night and seem to settle down when the baby reaches 5 to 6 months of age. Neurological damage appears to lead to disorganized behavior, hypersensitivity, and poor social connectedness.

Of importance to intervention programs is the fact that unless the newborns go through withdrawal at birth they are not identified in the hospital. Many hospitals rely on mothers' self-reporting of drug use, yet a survey in one Florida hospital found that only 27% of the pregnant women testing positive for drug use had admitted use (Bandstra, et al., 1989). Even testing for cocaine is of limited value because most tests can detect cocaine in the system for only 24 to 48 hours.

Central to the infant's emotional development are the interactive disorders that begin for the drug-exposed infant in the neonatal period. It is not difficult to understand how the hypersensitive infant makes normal family life difficult. The family must accommodate the infant's special needs by changing the family's normal patterns of behavior. The infant's incessant crying and disturbed sleep means that parents are exhausted and stretched to their limits. When their tolerance is exceeded, parents are more likely to take their frustration out on their infant, and the likelihood of abuse increases. Bonding with drug-exposed babies also may be difficult as the easily overstimulated infant will close his or her eyes, turn the head and howl when the caregiver attempts the normal social interaction of eye contact, talking, and smiling.

Difficulties become more apparent as the babies become older; for example, when children become 2 and 3 years old much more is expected of them. They are expected to be able to control their own behavior and to make increasing sense of the world. As the expectations increase, the drug-exposed child's damaged neurological system cannot keep pace, and the child's behavioral disorganization and temper tantrums become more extreme. The child appears to be difficult and "out of control" with frequent tantrums and outbursts of aggression.

This disorganization also is seen in play behavior. For example, it is expected that a 2 or 3 year old will be active, curious, and work hard to master the world around him or her. A cocaine-exposed 3 year old, however, has a flat, expressionless face, no interest in social interaction, and pays no attention to adult directives. The child is not likely to build, pretend, or engage others in his play. Toys are picked up and dropped, thrown, and battered. The child seldom talks, but over the course of an hour is likely to wind him- or herself up to higher and higher levels of frenetic activity that explodes in a tantrum that may go on for 20 minutes (Rodning, Beckwith, & Howard, 1989).

Because cocaine-exposed children are often poorly identified, it is important to recognize the types of problems they show during the preschool years. Cocaine-exposed children are likely to show some, but not all, of the following problems. In a continuation from infancy, preschoolers may show poor impulse control, irritability, poor goal-directed behavior, and a low tolerance for frustrating situations. They may be highly distractable, with attention spans as short as 5 seconds. They may have a low interest in social interaction, often insecure attachment, and expressive language difficulties. They are often hypersensitive to soft touch, with an inability to tolerate the feeling of restrictive winter clothes, seat belts, or having their hair combed. They may seem to crave rough physical play that overexcites them into tantrums. They ofter have poor spatial awareness, frequently bumping into things, walking off the edge of platforms, and showing no fear of heights. A high pain tolerance appears common; heat and pain do not appear to register in a normal manner.

The child does not learn from injuries and may need to be guarded from burning him- or herself on hot food, stoves, or radiators.

Although these problems are alarming at 36 months, they are more so by school age when the child may show an inability to self-initiate tasks, to set goals, to follow through on tasks. Because widespread crack abuse occurred 5 years ago, professionals are just beginning to see large numbers of these children in school. Initial reports suggest that these children are labelled as behavior problems and often show learning disabilities.

What Interventions Are Needed?

Organic deficits caused by prenatal drug exposure cannot be eliminated, but must be managed at each developmental stage. Following are specific suggestions for behavioral and environmental management techniques.

The behavioral techniques used with drug-exposed children are essentially the same as those used with many children with attention deficit or emotional disturbances. The immediate goal is to organize the child's environment to control the child's behavior. The long-term goal is to teach the child techniques to control his or her behavior. The following intervention techniques are useful for the specific behavioral disorders the child is showing.

1. *Teach soothing techniques and management of sleep disturbances.* For the easily overstimulated baby soothing, swaddling, quiet rocking, decreased stimulation, quiet, and calm handling (Dixon, Bresnahan, & Zuckerman 1990) are appropriate. Vertical rocking also has been found to be effective. Caregivers often make the mistake of using more than one soothing technique at a time, for example, rocking, singing, and patting the baby's back. Rather than calming the baby, using more than one technique at a time further overstimulates the child.

2. *Protect from overstimulation of an extremely active or noisy environment.* Because drug-exposed babies can overreact to different stimuli (social, auditory, tactile, visual) it is necessary to determine what they are reacting to. For example, professionals may wish to have caregivers keep records of what happens immediately before a tantrum to help determine the causes. They can help identify sources of environmental overload (e.g., trips to shopping center). They can also learn calm-down techniques (rocking, quiet room) and eventually help the child develop his or her own calm-down technique (remove self to quiet area, use rocking chair, suck thumb). With any of these techniques it is important to use verbal labels to help create awareness for the child, family, and caregiver of situations in which control is lost and needs to be reestablished. It is generally much easier to calm a child down before control is totally gone. If identified early, both child and caregiver can gain a sense that it is

possible to manage the behavior. Caregivers also need to be helped to label the situation as "this child is overloading" rather than "this is a bad child." Realizing that the behavior may be a result of neurological damage makes it easier for the caregiver to maintain control of his or her own emotions.

3. *Manage tactile defensiveness and overly rough play.* If a child is "tactically defensive," the feeling of wool, tight or restrictive clothes, having hair combed, or other types of touch that would be pleasant to most people, feels extremely unpleasant and invasive to them. Once this is recognized, the child's extreme tantrum at having to put on a particular pair of pants in the morning can be better understood and managed. In a similar manner, a child's desire for rough play may be recognized and watched so that the play does not degenerate into hitting, biting, or kicking behaviors.

4. *Work with the caregiver to minimize failures of attachment.* Caregivers of a withdrawn, avoidant, and irritable baby often play with the baby less and begin to leave the baby alone for longer periods without recognizing what they are doing. A first step toward breaking this cycle is to describe the baby's problem to the caregivers and explain the difficulty of interacting with such a baby. Such a discussion often removes the caregivers' guilt at not enjoying the baby and renews their energy to try to work with the child. It also helps to emphasize that even if an infant's responses are minimal, a baby wants and needs interactions that will gradually make him or her more socially responsive. Once this is understood, caregivers can be taught to cue in to the infant's social overload by introducing only one stimulus at a time. It is often necessary to experiment to find activities that the baby might enjoy.

5. *Help the child organize incoming information.* A fundamental characteristic of drug-exposed children is their disorganized patterns of thinking and reacting. This characteristic alone places a demand on their caregivers to provide a highly orderly, predictable, and organized environment for them. This means making a schedule, verbalizing it, and sticking to it. Making transitions will be difficult and are best managed by warning the child in advance and calmly letting him or her know what you expect him or her to do.

6. *Increase compliance and control tantrums.* Since toddlerhood is normally a period of negativism with intense tantrums, it is important to help the caregiver evaluate the situation to determine if the tantrums are within normal limits of behavior. Knowing that, many child management techniques used to increase cooperation are appropriate for use with drug-exposed children. For example, you can increase compliance by getting the child's attention before giving a command. This technique can

include making eye contact, touching the shoulder, and calling the child's name to make sure you have his or her attention before you tell the child what to do.

Because drug-exposed children's tantrums often are intense, caregivers frequently need to step back for 10 seconds to determine if the tantrum is due to manipulation (I want something) or neurological overload. You may be able to tell the difference between the two by looking at the situation and your reaction. If the child wants something and you have said no, and if your reaction is, "He is trying to control me," then it is likely to be a manipulative tantrum. If it is an overload tantrum, it is likely to be more intense, the cause is likely to be something that would not bother most children, and your reaction is more likely to be "He can't help it." In the latter case, it is important to be physically present with the child, avoid talking to him or her until the tantrum is over, and to eliminate the environmental irritant if possible. Some children escalate to the point that they frighten themselves and need a *calm* adult presence to help them regain control.

7. *Teach the child social cues and to use words rather than fighting to solve problems*. Because drug-exposed children have difficulty both with expressive language and in controlling their behavior, it is not too surprising that they tend to escalate problems with peers into hitting, biting, and scratching. Often they do not read social cues easily, failing to recognize that they are heading toward a conflict. It is important to help the child learn social cues by explaining what looks, gestures, and body language mean. The child also is helped if emotions are identified for him or her and if caregivers intervene early in altercations between children, modeling use of words rather than biting, pinching, and hitting.

Abused and Neglected Infants

Abused and neglected infants and children have typically experienced caregiving that is characterized by low rates of interaction, excessive threats and complaints, coupled with little affection, and few supportive reciprocal interactions (Burgess & Conger, 1977; Gaensbauer & Sands, 1979; Reid, Taplin, & Lorber, 1981). Maltreating parents tend to feel inadequate, find the care of their child an overwhelming burden, have a limited repertoire of disciplinary techniques, high family stress, and an abundance of mental health problems (Chapa, 1978; Green, 1976, 1985). In general, abusive parents show a pervasive pattern of poor functioning in the parental role. They frequently are not psychologically present for their children and offer their children little verbal or play stimulation. Abusing families also are characterized by high family discord and poor parental physical and mental health. Mothers and children in abusing families are caught in a negative spiral, with the mothers being less likely to engage the children in positive affectionate interactions, and the children more likely will fail to respond to the mother's attempts or to respond in an irritable manner (Wasserman, Green, & Allan 1983).

Abused and neglected preschoolers present a web of emotional and behavioral problems that create an enormous challenge to caregivers. Abused children often show neurological impairments and a large percentage display delayed cognitive, language, and social development (Martin, 1972). Kempe (1976) observed that abused children were anxious and fearful in interactions with adults; they expect punishment or criticism; and they are apathetic, showing an impaired capacity to play with peers or with toys. Their behavior may be characterized as depressed, unresponsive, negativistic, fearful, and with little interest in human contact (Green, 1985).

Abused infants under 6 months tend to be irritable; with a high-pitched cry and feeding difficulties (Kempe, 1976). Social and affective withdrawal are common, along with a tendency toward negative affect and weak attachment to parents and caregivers alike (Gaensbauer & Sands, 1979; George & Main, 1979). In day-care centers, abused children from 1 to 3 years of age are likely to physically assault their peers more often than do nonabused children. These young abused children are not likely to make friendly overtures to their caregivers and often harass them verbally or assault them physically (George & Main, 1979). In general, the abused infant and toddler's fearfulness and irritability in interactions with their parents are reenacted with other caregivers.

In day-care centers, there are some characteristic impairments that should be watched for in abused children (Augustinos, 1987; Green, 1985). These include:

- Preoccupation with external danger which deprives the children of the energy necessary for learning and mastery.
- A tendency to reenact the trauma by acting out the role of the "bad child" and seeking punishment from caregivers.
- A lack of basic trust which leads to detached and guarded relationships, low levels of communication, and anxious patterns of attachment.
- Identification with violent parents with resulting lack of impulse control, bullying, fighting, noncompliance, restlessness and hyperactivity.
- Poor self-concept because the child internalizes the displeasure the parents direct at him or her.

Without interventions to reverse serious emotional and intellectual impairments, abused children tend to perpetuate the cycle of abuse by reenacting the struggle with bad parents in each new relationship. Early intervention is necessary to prevent the abused child from perpetuating aggressive and provocative behavior in foster homes, school settings, and adult relationships (Green, 1985).

When professionals work with abused children, interventions are focused on changing undesirable child behavior and adult aggression. More specifically, interventions with abused children include:

1. *Encouraging the involvement of a primary caregiver.* Predictable and sensitive one-to-one interactions with adults are necessary to counteract fearfulness and mistrust.

2. *Providing appropriate play materials and activities.* Abused children whose homes contain appropriate play materials are able to obtain some gratification from interactions with the inanimate world that they are not consistently able to obtain from adults. Appropriate play materials promote exploratory interest, task involvement, and the child's feelings of competence.

3. *Identifying and modifying frustrating and difficult child behaviors.* An abused child expects that adults will punish him. Since these children know more about negative interactions than they do about positive interactions they will unconsciously work to set up negative situations with adults and with children. This means that they will keep breaking rules or teasing other children until they get the negative reactions they expect. Once caregivers understand what they are doing it is possible to break the negative cycle by enforcing the rules but refusing to be harsh, angry, or punitive.

Abused children also need to break their identification with their violent parents. They must be in an environment that will not allow bullying, fighting, or poor control of impulses. Repeatedly, they need to hear the message, "You are not a bad child; I know you are angry, but you may not hit him." They also need help to find acceptable ways of expressing their feelings through words, or to be removed from other children until they calm down.

5. *Providing verbal stimulation.* Abused children typically receive low levels of verbal stimulation and often need to "catch up" on their language skills. This situation means talking to the child about things he can see happening around him, labelling objects the child is interested in, and watching to see when the child seems to like to talk, that is, if there are few people around, if children are present, if adults are talking. Abused children commonly are delayed in expressive and receptive language as a result of impaired interpersonal relationships and low levels of verbalizations in their homes.

Infants Whose Parents Have Serious Social or Emotional Problems

Family conflict is both one of the most common and one of the most destructive influences on infant mental health (Block, Block, & Gierde, 1986; Emery, 1982; Schaffer, 1990). Family conflict in this context is not defined as the occasional disagreements and arguments that all families experience. Rather we are talking about conflict, mainly between parents, which is a pervasive style of interacting. This type of conflict is found in all social and economic classes, among those who function well in other areas of their adult lives, and often exists for years before there is a divorce in the family. It is the enduring nature of the conflict and discord that is damaging to children in the family. Through ongoing conflict, parents present to children a model of hostile and aggressive interpersonal relations that is the opposite of the way parents would like their children to behave. Even if parents do not actively attempt to involve the children in their conflicts, children will feel caught between two people to whom they are attached. Parents who are in conflict also present a powerful model of acting-out behavior, their tension may spill over into conflicts with their children, or they may be so preoccupied with their unhappiness that they are less emotionally responsive to their children (Schaffer, 1990).

In infancy, the effects of living in such a conflicted household are seen in symptoms of physical distress and bodily tension that often mirror the tension displayed by the adults. Thus, the infant may display inconsolable crying, bodily tension, and stomach upsets. An extreme example was seen in a month-old infant whose parents' conflict escalated into the father beating the mother. Hours later the previously healthy baby started regurgitating formula, and within a week was hospitalized with nonorganic failure to thrive. Two-year-olds in conflicted households show angry and noncompliant behaviors, 3-year-olds are likely to be physically restless and stubborn with rapidly shifting moods, and by 7 years of age aggressive, impulsive, and uncooperative behaviors begin and continue into adolescence (Block et al., 1986). In general, effects on the child take the form of aggressive and acting-out behaviors.

Disordered family relationships also are seen where one parent suffers from a mental illness. Maternal mental illness, in particular, places the infant and young child at high risk for mental health problems. Genetic studies have shown that children with one psychotic parent have a 12 to 16 times greater risk of psychiatric disorder than children who do not have a psychotic parent, with the risk rising to 40 times as great for those with two psychotic parents. The most common psychiatric condition, depression, affects nearly one quarter of mothers of preschool children.

The feelings common in depression (hopeless, helpless to change things, sadness, apathy) are evident among chronically deprived and impoverished mothers. Depression, of all psychiatric disturbances, poses the greatest risk for psychiatric disorder in children (Gotlib, 1989; Grunebaum & Cohler, 1982).

It is important to note here that while children of psychiatrically disturbed parents are at much higher risk, the majority of such children show no disturbance. The impact of parental psychosis varies with the number and timing of separations from the parent, with the quality of substitute care, with the degree of disruption in family functioning, and with the level of functioning of the other parent.

In their interactions with their mothers, the children of severely depressed parents show disturbances in attachment behavior and wide swings of mood that become more pronounced with advancing age. The infant may develop a primitive depressive state characterized by a sad face, withdrawal, failure to interact, and even refusal of food. Toddlers display difficulty with attachment behavior and wide swings in mood from happiness to abrupt rage. Slightly older children show disturbed interpersonal relations marked by conflict, instability, and dissatisfaction, as well as difficulties in handling emotions, particularly sadness and anger, and difficulty maintaining an emotional balance.

All of a child's risk is certainly not of a genetic origin. For children at high risk because one or both of their parents have genetically linked schizophrenia or depression, heredity is a necessary but not sufficient cause for their development of mental illness. Disorder in the environment in family relationships also is necessary. For example, mentally ill mothers often fail to engage their infants in interaction because they cannot read their baby's cues, are either withdrawn, intrusive, or over-controlling. Most mothers are able to read the emotions of joy, fear, anger, and sadness in their infants and to use this information to coordinate their interactions with their babies. When the baby has had too much interaction and looks away, most mothers are able to read the situation, pull back, and wait to reengage when the baby is ready. In the same way, mothers are able to see when the baby is able to do something for him- or herself and when assistance is necessary. These interactions teach the baby the power of communication, that adults can be trusted to help, and that they are powerful enough to do many things for themselves. Conversely, depressed mothers are more likely to display less positive affect, are angrier, more intrusive, and look away from their infants more often (Tronick, 1989). Because there is no basic communication of intent between the mother and infant, the baby fails to learn that his or her differential cries of hunger, boredom, and anger will be understood and responded to appropriately. The baby fails to develop basic trust that his or her needs will be met and becomes less interested in the social connection afforded by language. The baby expends so much energy attempting to establish harmony in interactions with the mother, but failing to do that, the baby comes to expect negative interpersonal interactions. Often the baby will withdraw from the interpersonal world and act as if there were no possibility of his or her affecting the object world. By the early preschool years such children show cognitive delays, attentional deficits, and poor persistence when tasks become even mildly difficult.

SUPPORTING FAMILIES

Rather than just focusing on the damage infants suffer, it is both important and hopeful to consider the infants and children who come through a host of damaging circumstances to function as adaptive and stable adults. These are the "resilient" children, those who despite the fact that they have so many things going against them, seem to be made strong by the difficulties they have experienced.

Children whose mental health survives intact despite their disadvantages are protected by factors in their environments and factors within themselves. Protective factors that reside within a child's physical makeup and temperament can include being physically strong, having a high activity level, and being socially engaging. Such children are less vulnerable to the impact of a hazardous environment than a physically weak, inactive, or withdrawn child. Werner (1990) described babies who were resilient despite exposure to multiple risks. They were the kind of babies who were, "very active, affectionate, cuddly, good-natured, and easy to deal with." They were children who were able to draw out affection and attention even from their overworked and over-stressed caregivers. Other protective factors in infancy include: alertness, being easy to calm, and being socially interested and active. Babies who do well despite serious difficulties in the first years have often had a relationship with one caregiver, not necessarily their mother, that was warm, responsive, and caring.

Resilient preschool children are both independent and highly responsive to people. They are active and involved in their play and tend to search their environments for new things to do, look at, and explore. These children would rather do things for themselves, but they also know when to ask adults or older children for necessary help. When in a difficult or high-stress situation these children continue to feel sure of themselves, are alert, and responsive. They are less likely to be anxious or to simply copy the behavior of those around them. They are willing to work on a problem or situation, feeling that eventually they will be able to solve it or make it better.

In terms of environmental factors, of key importance is having at least one person who provides stable care, affection, and attention during the first years. This key relationship allows children to develop trust in others and the secure sense that they are worthy of being loved. Grandparents and sibling caregivers often protect infants from long-term damage. Children of mothers who are mentally ill, single, in poverty, or teenagers themselves, often do best when grandparents provide care, emotional warmth, and financial assistance.

Sibling caregivers are another protection for high-risk infants. When mothers and other adult caregivers are stressed by social and personal problems, by their workloads and family responsibilities, the presence of sibling caregivers may have a positive impact on the entire family. When given extra attention by a sibling, an infant is likely to engage in more play and verbal interactions, may receive the affection and attention that the adults in the family are unable to give, and may form a primary attachment to that sibling. In turn, the children who help care for their infant siblings are likely to be more responsible and nurturing in their behavior toward their siblings and their peers.

Just as a sibling can supplement the care of overextended caregivers, friends and playmates can serve as an extra source of emotional support for children in dysfunctional families. Close friends and their families allow children to see different ways in which families operate and cope with their problems. They may also allow such children a place to take shelter from the chaos or difficulties in their own homes.

There also are ways of caring for or raising children that tend to increase their adaptability (Schaffer, 1990). These general orientations toward raising children come into play in infancy and are important throughout the school years. Boys appear to do best and are most resilient when they are raised in families that have more rules, structure, parental supervision, a male role model, and where the expression of their feelings is encouraged. Girls appear to do best where they are not overprotected, where they are encouraged to be independent and to take risks, when they receive consistent emotional support from their primary caregiver, and when their mother is consistently employed.

MODELS OF INTERVENTION

Unchangeable risks may be thought of as those factors in the child's life that, although detrimental to social or emotional well-being, are changeable only at extraordinary social or monetary costs. Examples of these factors are conditions of poverty, the size of the family, or the fact that there is only one adult caregiver. Among changeable factors are: parental

caregiving behaviors, quality of language stimulation, and adult understanding of the child's emotional needs. In the infant and young child,
factors that both facilitate resiliency and are potentially changeable include: communication skills, problem solving and self-help skills, feelings
of autonomy, self-esteem, and loss of control. Between these two ex-
tremes are those risk factors that may be "managed" even if they may not
be changed directly. Among these manageable factors are those of the
child's temperament, activity level, social orientation, and physical
strength. Each level of risk carries its own programmatic demands: the
unchangeable factors may be used to screen those children who are at
highest risk for mental health problems. Manageable factors such as birth
conditions and temperament may be written into variations in curriculum
that are designed to address the needs of individual children. The changeable behaviors in the family and child are often the primary focus of
program efforts.

Werner (1990) draws some important implications from high-risk
young children.

- Intervention services should focus first on the most vulnerable infants in any high-risk category; those who lack the essential social
  support, love, and affection that serve to protect children from negative influences.
- When assessing the situation of infants, professionals need to consider not only the risk factors but also the strengths and the supportive factors that already exist in the community or that can be
  brought to bear on the situation.
- Often when the parents cannot adequately care for an infant other
  significant people can be found in the infant's life: grandparents,
  siblings, and caring friends who can play a role in helping the child.
- For any intervention to be effective, the child must be able to trust
  that the help, affection, and support will be there consistently. The
  child needs to be able to know that he or she will continue to be
  accepted despite any shortcomings.
- Infants and young children are better able to cope with stress and
  adversity if at least parts of their lives are organized and predictable,
  with rules and limits that are consistently enforced.
- Although it is clear that some children are biologically more resistant
  to stress than others, the resilience of most children can be improved
  if they are helped to learn independence, flexible problem solving,
  self-confidence, and trust in the people around them.

Although infant mental health is a long way from being routinely
included in intervention programs, much progress has been made in the
past few years. The emotional problems of infants have been recognized
and described. Many effective intervention techniques are available. The

growing interest in this topic will help ensure that when professionals work to help the "whole child," the child's emotional needs will be included in the planning.

REFERENCES

Augustinos, M. (1987). Developmental effects of child abuse: Recent findings. *Child Abuse and Neglect, 11*, 15-27.

Bandstra, E. S., Steele, B.W., Burkett, G.T., Palow, D.C., Levandoski, N., & Rodriguez, V. (1989). Prevalence of perinatal cocaine exposure in an urban multi-ethnic population. *Pediatric Research, 26*, 20-36.

Barron, A.P., & Earls, F. (1984). The relation of temperament and social factors to behavior problems in three-year-old children. *Journal of Child Psychology and Psychiatry, 25*, 23-33.

Besharov, D.J. (1990). Crack children in foster care. *Children Today, 19 (4)*, 21-25.

Block, J.H., Block, J., & Gierde, P.F. (1986). The personality of children prior to divorce: A prospective study. *Child Development, 57*, 827-840.

Burgess, R.L., & Conger, R.D. (1977). Family interaction patterns related to child abuse and neglect: Some preliminary findings. *Child Abuse and Neglect, 1*, 269-277.

Chapa, D. (1978). *The relationship between child abuse/neglect and substance abuse contrasting Mexican-American and Anglo families. Interim report.* San Antonio, TX: San Antonio Child Abuse Project Civic Organization.

Chavkin, W., & Kandall, S.R. (1990). Between a rock and a hard place: Perinatal drug abuse. *Pediatrics, 85*, 223-225.

Chess, S., & Thomas, A. (1987). *Know your child.* New York: Basic Books.

Dixon, S.D., Bresnahan, K., & Zuckerman, B. (1990). Cocaine babies: Meeting the challenge of management. *Contemporary Pediatrics, 1 (2)*, 70-92.

Department of Health and Human Services, Office of Evaluation and Inspections. (1990, June). *Crack Babies.* Washington, DC: U.S. Government Printing Office.

Emery, R.E. (1982). Interpersonal conflict and the children of discord and divorce. *Psychological Bulletin, 92*, 310-330.

Ferber, R. (1985). *Solve your child's sleep problems.* New York: Simon & Schuster.

Finnegan, L.P. (1982). Substance abuse: Implications for the newborn. *Pediatric Nursing, 91*, 17-23.

Gaensbauer, T.J., & Sands, K. (1979). Distorted communications in abused/neglected infants and their potential impact on caregivers. *Journal of American Academy of Child Psychiatry, 18*, 236-250.

George C., & Main, M. (1979). Social interactions of young abused children: Approach, avoidance, and aggression. *Child Development, 50*, 306-318.

Gotlib, I.H. (1989). Interpersonal aspects of depression. *The Harvard Medical School Mental Health Letter, 6* (4), 24-26.

Green, A.H. (1976). A psychodynamic approach to the study and treatment of child abusing parents. *Journal of the American Academy of Child Psychiatry, 15*, 414–429.

Green, A.H. (1985). Child abuse and neglect. In D. Schaffer, A.A. Ehrhardt, & L.L. Greenhill (Eds.), *Clinical guide to child psychiatry* (pp. 315–335). New York: Free Press.

Gruenbaum, H., & Cohler, B.J. (1982). Children of parents hospitalized for mental illness: Attentional and interactional studies. *Journal of Children in Contemporary Society, 15*, 43–55.

Howard, J., Beckwith, L., Rodning, C., & Kropenske, V. (1989, June). The development of young children of substance-abusing parents: Insights from seven years of intervention and research. *Zero to Three*, 12–14.

Kempe, R. (1976). Arresting or freezing the developmental process. In R.E. Helfer & C.H. Kempe (Eds.), *Child abuse and neglect, the family and community* (pp. 67–73). Cambridge, MA: Ballinger.

Martin, H.P. (1972). The child and his development. In C.H. Kempe & R.E. Helfer (Eds.), *Helping the battered child and his family* (pp. 25–73). Philadelphia: J.B. Lippincott.

Reid, J.B., Taplin, P., & Lorber, R. (1981). A social interactional approach to the treatment of abusive families. In R.B. Stuart (Ed.), *Violent behavior: Social learning approaches to prediction, management, and treatment*. New York: Brunner/Mazel.

Rodning, C., Beckwith, L., & Howard, J. (1989). Characteristics of attachment organization and play organization in prenatally drug-exposed toddlers. *Development and Psychopathology, 1*, 277–289.

Schaffer, H.R. (1990). *Making decisions about children. Psychological questions and answers*. Oxford, England: Basil Blackwell.

Stern, (1985). *The interpersonal world of the infant*. New York: Basic Books.

Turecki, S. (1985). *The difficult child*. New York: Bantam Books.

Tronick, E.Z. (1989). Emotions and emotional communication in infants. *American Psychologist, 44* (2), 112–119.

Wasserman, G., Green, A., & Allen, R. (1983). Going beyond abuse: Maladaptive patterns of interaction in abusing mother-infant pairs. *Journal of the American Academy of Child Psychiatry, 22*, 245–252.

Werner, E.E. (1990). Protective factors and individual resilience. In S.J. Meisels & J.P. Shonkoff (Eds.), *Handbook of early childhood intervention* (pp. 97–116). Cambridge, England: Cambridge University Press.

Williamson, G.G., & Zeitlin, S. (in press). *Coping in young children: Early intervention to enhance development and adaptive behavior*. Baltimore: Brookes.

Chapter 3

Meeting the Needs of Special Populations

NOMA B. ANDERSON
LEMMIETTA G. McNEILLY

The field of early intervention is facing many challenges in meeting the needs of special populations. Many practitioners feel ill-prepared to plan appropriate assessment and inteventinon programs to an increasing number of families wiht whom they work. Much of traditional educational preparation has been monocultural in perspective, idealistic in presentation, and has dealt too little with the harsh realities of the lives of many families with infants and toddlers who are disabled or at risk. Early intervention services with infants and young children must be provided within the context of the family, and its strengths and needs. P. L. 99-457 requires early interventionists to function within the philosophical framework of family centered care, which programs care and intervention in the context of the family's lifestyle and needs (Shelton, Jeppson, & Johnson, 1989). When working with nonmainstream families, or special populations, early interventionists must also do so within the context of families' values and priorities.

This chapter addresses three special populations that present challenges to early intervention practitioners. These are: (1) families from culturally diverse populations, (2) low-income families, (3) HIV-positive infants and their families.

ADDRESSING THE NEEDS OF THE CULTURALLY DIVERSE

Of all the new developments that have arisen within the field of early intervention, few are more challenging than meeting the needs of children and families from culutrally diverse populations. Historically, P. L. 94-142, and more recently P. L. 99-457, require that early interventionists serve children with disabilities and at-risk children in culturally sensitive and culturally appropriate programs.

It is important for the professional to be socioculturally competent regarding the influence that sociocultural factors can bear on the developmental process. For these professionals to work effectively with families from ethrolinguistically diverse populations, they must have an understanding of cultural values and how diffierent cultural groups view health and disabilities.

Cultural Beliefs and Values

It is important to keep in mind that there is considerable diversity in cultural groups, and the extent to which any family can be characterized by any set of cultural values and practices varies with each individual family. There are several cultural beliefs and values that may reveal cross-cultural differences between Anglo-American ethnics groups and many ethnolinguistically diverse groups.

Cross-cultural differences can occur between Anglo-American families and families from ethnolinguistically diverse populations. One such difference is the contrast between fatalism versus personal control over the environment. Personal control over the environment is a traditional middle-class Anglo-American philosophy characterized by the belief that one controls one's destiny, that one has control over one's life and experiences. Many mainstream faimilies adopt this cultural view which manifests itself as assertive entry into and utilization of service delivery systems. given that their infant child has been identified as having some type of disability or at-risk condition, many families recognize the improtance of appropriate professionals assessing the child and providing intervention. Even though families often experience feelings of anger, shock, and denial, many recognize the need for early intervention professionals and programs. Public Law 99-457 was conceived in a philosophical value system that views parents as partners with early intervention professionals. They are expected to be active participants in planning intervention goals and in implementing early intervention programming. They also are expected to actively seek out and select the services that early intervention programs provide.

In contrast to active and assertive participation, many families from ethnolinguistically diverse populations may have a fatalistic philosophy manifested by (1) acceptance of the fact that their child is disabled, and (2) a sense of personal responsibility for the care of the young child. Being a fatalist often promotes a different mode of participation in the early intervention process. For example, many families from ethnolinguistically diverse populations first may turn to the family for support and advice. Others first may turn to familiar and trusted community resources such as the church and community respected "lay practitioners" or the conventional, culturally appropriate, medical practitioners. The pattern of entering and accessing the eraly intervention system from a fatalistic view may, therefore, be different from the assertive, taking control way of many Anglo-American families. In summary, many non-Anglo families may not interact with professionals as partners in the early intervention process.

An orientation to the past versus a future orientation is a second difference in cultural beliefs and values between Anglo-American families and families from ethnolinguistically diverse populations. The Anglo-American cultural view is characterized as future oriented (Schilling & Brannon, 1986). Accordingly, the philosophical foundation for early identification and early intervention is based on a future orientation. The justification, the raison d'état, for early intervention programming and the costs of early intervention, as required by P. L. 99-457, is the improved functioning and quality of life that lies ahead for the child and the family. The philosophy of early intervention is, therefore, based on the Anglo-American future-oriented world view that considers the present as preparation for the future.

In contrast, many non-Anglo families share the cultural orientation of viewing the present as a consequence of the past. Tradition is important, thus many non-Anglo families may have greater confidence in following tradonal practices and customs than in following unfamiliar cultural practices. The past orientation is closely tied to the fatalistic world view. Viewing a disability as God's will, or viewing a disability as punishment or a sign of past misdeeds, are views held by some families from non-Anglo cultures. Goal setting, formulating short- and long-term goals, planning annual goals and intervention programs for the child and the family, as P. L. 94-142 and P. L. 99-457 require, are based on a future orientation, a familiar orientation for many Anglo-American families. However, the rationale and the procedures for program planning and goal setting may not be as evident and self-explanatory to non-Anglo families who are not as invested in a future-oriented world view.

A third cross-cultural difference involves human equality versus hierarchy, rank, and status (Schilling & Brannon, 1986). Equalitarianism is a part of the philosophical foundation of the United States. Accordingly, in many Anglo-American families, there is a equalitarian relationship between adult family members. Similarly, many middle-class Anglo-American families feel comfortable with an equalitarian relationship with early intervention and health care professionals. Public Law 99-457 incorporated such a philosophical perspective by making parents partners with the professionals in the early intervention process. The role of parents in the Individualized Family Services Plan (IFSP) process is fundamentally based on a human equality cultural perspective.

Hierarchy, rank, and protocol characterize many non-Anglo cultures and also many families from such cultures. There may not be an immediate desire in these parents to be "partners" with their young child's early intervention and health care providers. Accordingly, many families from traditional ethnolinguistically diverse populations may not be immediately participatory in the goal formulation and implementation phases of intervention as the professionals may anticipate. Many non-Anglo families may feel more comfortable with professional "distancing" than do many Anglo-American families. Family roles and responsibilities show a great deal of cultural diversity in that in many cultures there is hierarchical relationships within the family. For example, in some Asian-American families, there may be a strong adherence to hierarchy, protocol, and deference to authority (Dillard, 1983). In many traditional Mexican-American families there is a sense of hierarchy within the family, with the hierarchy transcending from the grandparents, to the parents, to the children.

A fourth cross-cultural value difference involves beliefs, attitudes, and practices regarding health, illness, and disability (Anderson & Fenichel, 1989). For the most part, Anglo-American families accept the medical model regarding etiologies of disabilities and conventional health practices accepted by the Anglo-American health care system. A great deal of diversity exists among many families from non-Anglo cultures regarding disability and health. Many traditional Asian-American families hodl that congenital birth disabilities may be viewed as punishments for sins committed by ancestors, or because the pregnant mother did not avoid places and situations where harmful spirits exist. Among some traditional Hispanic families, health and disability are closely intertwined with religion; for example, a person must be in tune with God to maintain good health. Illness and disability are viewed as imbalances between "hot" and "cold," with treatment seeking to correct the impalance. A similar dichotomy is part of the traditional Asian-American perspective of health, illness, and treatment. The yin-yang system is somewhat similar to a hot-cold dichotomy. Good health and the absence of disability depend on maintaining a balance within the body between the opposing forces of yin and yang (Randall-David, 1989). Yin is the passive or negative force that is always complementary to and contrasted with yang, the active or positive force.

There is a dynamic interaction between a family's cultural beliefs, the family's values, experiences and expectations, childrearing and management practices, and the young child's development. For early intervention professionals to work effectively with infants, toddlers, and families from ethnolinguistically diverse populations they must gain an understanding and awareness of cultural diversity. Such sociocultural competence is now a best practices requirement for early interventionists since the demographics of America are changing so dramatically. One significant change is that the number of non-Anglo individuals is increasing, with a great amount of the increase in the numbers occurring among those who are younger than 18 years of age. Early interventionists must, therefore, strive for increased cultural sensitivity toward cultures different from their own.

These changing demograhics have significant impact on the field of eary intervention. Hanson, Lynch, and Wayman (1990) present the following demograhic projections:

- Of the infants born in the United States in 1984, 36% were born to ethnolinguistically diverse families. It is projected that by the year 2000, 38% of the children under the age of 18 will be from ethnolinguistically diverse families.
- Compared to 1985, in the year 2000 there will be 2.4 million more Hispanic children, 1.7 million more African-American children, 483,000 more children of other ethnic groups, and 66,000 more Anglo children.
- By the year 2030, compared to 1985, there will be 5.5 million more Hispanic children, 2.6 million more African-American children, 1.5 million more children from other ethnic groups, and 6.2 million fewer Anglo children.
- Using a very conservative estimate, 3% of these infants and toddlers will be disabled, and a much larger group will be at risk for disabilities.

Hanson, Lynch, and Wayamn (1990) stress that gaining cultural competence requires systematic observation of cultures, observations that are ethnographic in nature. These authors present six aspects of ethnographic information that the professional should know about the community with which he or she is working.

- Describe the ethnic group with which the family identifies; for example, the family's country of origin, language, and size of the ethnic community in your city.

- Identify the social organization of the ethnic community, what organizations or individuals have formal and informal leadership roles, and what resources are available in the ethnic community.
- Describe the prevailing belief system in the ethnic community; for example, values, ceremonies, and symbols important to that culture.
- Become informed about the history of the ethnic group and current events that directly and indirectly affect the family.
- Determine how members of the community gain access to and utilize social services.
- Identify the attitudes of the ethnic community toward seeking early intervention.

TARGETING SERVICES TO LOWER-INCOME FAMILIES

In 1985 Cole and Anderson wrote:

> Poverty and handicapping conditions can each be defined by the same formula: the difference between "what is" and "what ought to be." To be either poor or handicapped is to be disadvantaged. But the burdens imposed by being poor *and* handicapped can have a cumulative impact. (p. 61)

Many consider the low-income family to be a special population because of the array of needs that the family may have, because of the reliance of the family on targeted educational and federal assistance programs, and because of the values and priorities that the family possesses.

Non-Anglo families constitute a large proportion of America's low-income families. Edmunds, Martinson, and Goldberg (1990) present the following disturbing facts about children from families that are poor and non-Anglo:

- Of children under the age of three, 23.3% are poor; 17.3% of Anglo children under the age of three are poor; 50.4% of African-American children under the age of three are poor; 43.6% of Hispanic children under the age of three are poor.
- Of children under the age of 18, 19.2% are poor; 14.1% of Anglo children under the age of 18 are poor; 43.5% of African-American children under the age of 18 are poor; 37.6% of Hispanic children under the age of 18 are poor.
- Of the 15.3 million Anglo children under the age of six in the United States in 1987—70% of all children under six—2.1 million were poor. Of the remaining 30% of children of color under six, 2.9 million were poor, making the proportion of young children of color who live in poverty far higher than their Anglo peers.
- In 1987, 46% of female-headed families with children and approximately 60% of female-headed families with preschool-age children were poor.

- Child support amounts are lowest for the less educated, never married, and non-Anglo.

- Households with children under 18 years of age headed by African-American or Hispanic women are one-and-a-half times as likely to be in poverty as those headed by Anglo women.

- About 24% of Anglo families are headed by 15- to 24-year-olds who live in poverty, compared to 38% for Hispanics and 57% for African-Americans. Forty-seven percent of these Hispanic poor families and 75% of these African-American poor families are headed by single women.

- Between 1980 and 1987, the median income of children living in single-parent families declined by 19%.

- In 1988, 20% of all children had no form of public or private insurance, compared to 17% in 1982.

These statistics about the nation's poor children are important to understand because poverty places children at risk for disabilities and developmental delay. The affect of low income and poverty on infants and toddlers who are disabled and their families is severe, for poverty imposes a number of barriers that limit the family's access, awareness, and utilization of the educational and health care systems. Mothers of low-income families often experience inadequate prenatal care. Poor maternal health is associated with prematurity, infant malnutrition, low birth weight infants, and growth retardation. Low birth weight infants are at greater risk for brain damage, mental retardation, learning disabilities, cerebral palsy, and developmental delay (Avery, 1984; Cole & Anderson, 1985). For many children from low-income families, early identification and early intervention do not occur or are inconsistently provided. This situation constitutes serious neglect of a large segment of the nation's families. Poor children are more at risk for accidental or traumatic injury, higher doses of lead in their environment, and prenatal exposure to drugs, alcohol, and AIDS than middle-class children. Because a relationship has been found to exist between poverty, disabling conditions, and learning problems, children from low-income families also become high risks for school failure (Edmunds, Martinson, & Goldberg, 1990).

Malnutrition and growth retardation are serious problems among low-income children. The prevalence of iron and protein anemia and vitamin deficiencies among poor American children due to inadequate diets is high (Bullough & Bullough, 1982; Cole & Anderson, 1985). The lack of nutritional food, nutritional counseling, medical help, and immunizations available to low-income families is of such concern that the federal program, Women, Infants, and Children (WIC), was created to address these needs. Yet, it is reported that WIC is able to serve less than 50% of the high-risk, low-income, eligible population (Edmunds, Martinson, &

Goldberg, 1990). One reason for the limited impact of WIC is that the number of low-income families and the cost of food have dramatically increased and, even though WIC funding has increased, the amount of federal funding is inadequate to meet these growing needs. Those families that are served receive much-needed support and services. Low-income families are a special population because they are an underserved population whose health care and educational needs often are not consistently and comprehensively addressed. In addition to the WIC program, there are numerous programs that provide assistance to low-income families with children who are disabled.

Medicaid is a federally supported and state-administered assistance program that provides medical care for low-income individuals and families (Frattali & White, 1988). Each state decides what services it will provide and who is eligible for coverage; therefore, services supported by the Medicaid programs vary considerably from state to state. Currently, all states (except Arizona) and the District of Columbia have Medicaid programs. Medicaid's eligibility provisions are among the most complex of assistance programs because of its interrelatedness with two federal cash assistance programs, Aid to Families with Dependent Children (AFDC) and Supplementary Security Income (SSI), and because of its varied state regulations. There are concerns regarding the capability of these programs to adequately address the needs of low-income families. Edmunds, Martinson, and Goldberg (1990) report that the number of poor children who received AFDC assistance declined from 73% in 1975 to 56% in 1987.

Early and Periodic Screening, Diagnosis, and Treatment (EPSDT), a component of Medicaid, is a program that was created to provide preventive and coordinated medical care to children of low-income families. The EPSDT program is the nation's single largest federal program providing health care to children who are poor. EPSDT goes beyond the reimbursement function of Medicaid by ensuring the provision of services to eligible children (Cole & Anderson, 1985). In 1989, however, the U.S. Department of Health and Human Services reported that only 34% of the 10.5 million children eligible for Medicaid received EPSDT services (Edmunds, Martinson, & Goldberg, 1990). It has been suggested that EPSDT legislation needs to change so that more low-income children can be cared for, and the program can be utilized to its full potential. As a result of these suggestions, in 1989, congressional changes were made to increase the frequency of screening examinations to identify children's preventable health problems; to improve children's entry into the health care system; to improve provider participation; and to expand the package of diagnostic and treatment services entitled under the EPSDT program (White, 1990). The screening services mandated under EPSDT are a comprehensive health and developmental history, a comprehensive unclothed physical examination, immunizations, laboratory tests, and health education. Hearing services, speech-language pathology services, augmentative communication devices, and physical and occupational therapy are also provided under the EPSDT program. Although the new provision became effective April 1, 1990, it may take 5 to 10 years for the Health Care Financing Administration to enforce the changes and for all states to implement the improvements.

Services for Children With Special Health Care Needs (formerly Crippled Children's Services) is a program that provides ongoing care to children with a chronic disability (Cole & Anderson, 1985). This program provides acute medical treatment for specific handicapping conditions and also provides long-term management including planning individualized care, counseling, coordinating services, patient status monitoring, and periodic reassessment. Eligibility and specific services vary from state to state.

Head Start is a program designed to help preschool children from low-income families. In 1974, Congress enacted legislation which mandated that at least 10% of the total number of children enrolled in Head Start programs in each state be disabled and that services be provided to meet their special needs (Cole & Anderson, 1985). The disability categories recognized by Head Start are visual impairment, deafness, hearing impairment, orthopedic handicap, speech-language impairment, mental retardation, health impairment, emotional disturbance, and learning disabilities.

Finally, P. L. 94-142 and its amendments, such as P. L. 99-457, ensure that early identification and services be provided to all children who are disabled from birth to age 21 (Cole & Anderson, 1985).

Concerns about the quality of early identification and early intervention services provided to low-income families continue to exist, even though the federal assistance programs were created for this purpose. Edmunds, Martinson, and Goldberg (1990) report on a 1988 study conducted by the Robert Wood Johnson Foundation's Collaborative Study of Children with Special Needs to examine the effect of P. L. 94-142 in five metropolitan school districts, which concluded that gaps in access to health care in the communities they studied continue to exist for poor children and for non-Anglo children, and that the impact of P. L. 94-142 is lessened in those states that have weak Medicaid, mental health, child service agencies, and EPSDT programs. Another finding of this study was that the age at which a child's disability is identified is in direct correlation to the mother's educational level, in that the more education the mother has, the earlier the child's disability is identified.

Even though there are a number of programs for children who are disabled and from low-income families, there continue to be serious problems in the access and delivery of health care to low-income families. Low-income families continue to be a seriously underserved population because (1) federal and state funding has been unable to meet the increasing needs of the increasing numbers of low-income families; (2) there is nationwide inconsistency in the provision of early identification and early intervention services to children who are poor and disabled and their families (e.g., some programs and some states provide alternative/augmentative communication devices and others do not); (3) gaps and overlaps exist in services that are provided by educational and health assistance programs; (4) the health care system is a complicated maze of bureaucracy for low-income families to conquer; and (5) prior to implementation of P. L. 99-457 early intervention services were poorly coordinated, in that they were frequently provided at a number of different facilities by various agencies and professionals.

Sullivan (1991), Secretary of the U.S. Department of Health and Human Services, asserts that the principal issue relating to health care for the poor is access: lack of access to health care and lack of financial access to health care. He goes on to state:

> The answer to improved access for the poor has to lie in federal, state, and local programs targeted to the conditions and needs of the poor; in redefined priorities, favoring access and delivery; in consensus development and coalition building around the effective integration of services and management of care . . . All Americans should have needed health care. The road to reform must include providing effective access to an expanded system. (p. 10)

An important variable regarding low-income families with children who are disabled and the delivery of adequate health and educational services is the sociocultural factors that relate to poverty. Many of the cultural values and behaviors that are discussed when describing ethnolinguistically diverse populations also can be used to describe low-income families. Because of the many needs that these families have, a fatalistic versus a personal control over one's environment, and a present versus a future orientation can characterize many low-income families.

Another difference that may be found between low-income families and middle-class families concerns the importance of time versus the importance of human interaction (Schilling & Brannon, 1986). Strict adherence to time is a mainstream custom that is not shared by many nonmainstream populations. Human interaction can be more important than time. Schilling and Brannon write that families and early intervention professionals may differ on the value of time in that most professionals are ruled by time and schedules, but many low-income families are not as rigid about appointment times.

Another possible difference between low-income families and middle-class families is in patterns of utilization and preferences for health care. Many middle-class parents readily and immediately seek the professional assistance of early intervention professionals and health care providers given the suspicion of a problem. Many low-income families rely first on family members, community practitioners, and community members for advice, identification, diagnosis, and treatment. There is often mistrust, lack of confidence, and suspicion of mainstream educational and health care providers because these professionals are not part of the family's cultural group or are unfamiliar with the family's cultural group. Quite often families from low-income ethnolinguistically diverse populations filter the counseling and instructions given them by mainstream professionals through their particular cultural belief and value system.

In conclusion, effective early intervention with low-income families must consider the obstacles, prejudices, hardships, and discrimination experienced by these families. Early identification and early intervention strategies must include creative planning so that infants' and toddlers' health and educational care is provided in the context of:

- Family centered care
- Comprehensive care settings
- Community-based settings
- Socioculturally sensitive programming
- Professionals who treat the family with respect and dignity.

HIV-POSITIVE INFANTS AND THEIR FAMILIES

The Public Health Service has estimated that in 1991, 3,200 children will have AIDS, and approximately 10,000 to 20,000 children will be born with congenital human immunodeficiency virus (HIV) infection, which is the cause of acquired immune deficiency syndrome (AIDS). Contrary to popular belief and early reports, these children are living past the age of two and attend school. These children are at risk for developmental delays due to a number of factors. Professionals employed in early intervention programs who work with children who are developmentally disabled need to be cognizant of the developmental and physiological changes that HIV-positive children may display.

The Centers for Disease Control's (1991) statistics regarding pediatric HIV infection rates indicate that approximately 1,800 out of 6,000 babies born to women who test positive for the HIV virus acquire the virus.

Fortunately, all babies born to HIV-positive mothers do not test positive for the HIV virus after the mother's antibodies are no longer present in the babies' blood. Pediatric AIDS is another problem that is related to drug abuse. Results of a 1987 New York City study of infants who tested positive for AIDS antibodies indicated that 1 in 62 infants were seropositive, that is, when they were given the HIV blood test these children presented with antibodies against the virus in their blood, meaning they had been exposed to the infection. The common source of exposure was intravenous drug use either by the mother or her sexual partner (Jones & Lopez, 1988).

HIV is the human immunodeficiency virus that causes AIDS. It affects 30 to 50% of infants born to mothers who are HIV positive, and it affects children from all cultural groups, socioeconomic levels, family structures, and regions of the country. A significant number of women of childbearing age have acquired the HIV virus and may pass it on to their children while breast feeding. The majority of the children with HIV infection are born to mothers who were intravenous drug users (IVDUs) or mothers who were sexual partners of IVDUs. A disproportionate number of these women and their children are African-Americans and members of low socioeconomic groups. Fifty-one percent are African-American, 28% Anglo, and 20% Hispanic. (Guinan & Hardy, 1987). Of reported children under the age of 5 years, 56% are African-American and 26% are Hispanic (Crocker & Cohen, 1990).

Transmission of the HIV

Young children with the HIV virus acquire it congenitally from their HIV-infected mothers. The mothers became infected by exposure to infected blood, contaminated needles shared during intravenous drug use, and by sexual contact with men who were infected. Approximately 40 to 50% of the infants born to infected mothers become infected (Crocker & Cohen, 1990).

Another route by which children acquire the HIV virus is the infusion of contaminated blood or blood products. Infection derived from sexual activity, sexual abuse, or the intravenous use of street drugs also exists, but at unknown low levels in children below 13 years of age. The Centers for Disease Control reports that blood-related AIDS represents 16% of the total for children and 9% for adolescents and adults. Two thirds of these instances represent the use of blood in a variety of medical situations, particularly for small premature infants, surgical patients, and those with various hematologic disorders requiring transfusion, treated in the period from 1978–1985. The remaining one third of children have hemophilia.

Implications for Acquired HIV Infection

The implications regarding early intervention services for infants, toddlers, and young children with acquired HIV infection are less predictable than in the congenital form. Once children develop the symptomatic disease the course resembles that in adults. The intrusive encephalopathy seen in infants and toddlers is not found in children, although infections and tumors of the central nervous system can occur. Serious chronic illness is assuredly present, with all of its potential interference with normal childhood progress. A significant factor is the effect that HIV positivity has on the individual's morale and belief in self, with developmental implications. Also, when involvement with the virus becomes known to others, discrimination and social isolation can be intense. A final concern is the risk of a man with hemophilia and HIV infection passing this to his spouse in sexual contact, and ultimately to potential unborn children.

DESCRIPTION OF THE CONGENITAL HIV-POSITIVE CHILD

Pediatric HIV-positive infants, toddlers, and school-age children generally have intelligent minds, wants, desires and needs similar to healthy children. Of reported children (Crocker & Cohen, 1990) 82% are under 5 years of age, many are under 2 years of age, particularly those with early involvement. However, they are infected and are susceptible to other viral infections. The newborns are generally unremarkable except for those who present with drug effects or addiction. The antibody levels in the mother and newborn reveal the mother's exposure to the HIV virus.

Most HIV-positive children do not live with their biological mothers. In some cases the mothers of these children have already died of AIDS. In other situations, drug-addicted mothers abandoned their infants at birth or soon after. Others may be removed from the home by child protective services because of neglect. HIV-positive children are not relegated to any one region of the United States. However, 15 urban areas account for 63% of the pediatric population (Crocker & Cohen, 1990). These children live in houses and apartments, and some are homeless. Unfortunately, some live in hospitals or foster homes designed particularly for babies who test positive for the HIV virus.

Physiological Changes

As of January 1990, the Centers for Disease Control reported that 2,055 infants and children under age 13 had been reported with AIDS. The Public Health Service estimated that in the next 5 years, HIV may become the largest infectious cause of mental retardation and encephalopathy in children under age 13. The incidence of central nervous system dysfunction in infants and children with symptomatic HIV infection ranges from 78 to 90% in various studies (Diamond & Cohen, 1989). HIV infection of the central nervous system may produce progressive encephalopathy, characterized by loss of developmental milestones, intellectual deficits, and impaired brain growth.

An infant born to a mother who is HIV positive has a multiplicity of needs including clinical, developmental, housing, nutrition, health, education, environmental, social, and emotional concerns. They may appear healthy, displaying no symptoms or associated illness, or they may possess developmental delays requiring early intervention services. All infants born to mothers with HIV infection are at environmental risk for developing delays. The truly infected infants are at biological and established risk for developmental disorders.

Congenital HIV infection has an insidious effect on the central nervous system. This characteristic "encephalopathy" can be anticipated in the vast majority of children with symptomatic infection. The basis appears to be a direct involvement of the virus in the brain, resulting in changes in the blood vessels and loss of brain mass. An increasing acquired "microcephaly," or failure of the head to grow at the expected rate is usual.

Most infants with the virus begin to show clinical symptoms in the first year of life. The most common symptoms include poor weight gain, high incidence of bacterial infection, pernicious pulmonary infections, chronic diarrhea, and delayed development. About 60% will have related illness by 1 year of age, and another 20% by 2 years of age. Certain children, however, have asymptomatic HIV infection for many years with no specific problems except for persistence of antibodies that indicate sustained presence of the virus. Presently the median survival time for children with congenital HIV infection is about 4 years of age; certain reports have noted 30% mortality by 2 years of age, and 60% by 5 years. The major study centers have experienced individual survivals well into the school years, and even to the early teens (Crocker & Cohen, 1990).

Developmental Patterns

The incidence of developmental disabilities in children with HIV infection has been observed to be as high as 90% (Belman, et al., 1988). They may have global developmental delays, isolated cognitive deficits, a precipitous or gradual loss of previously acquired skills such as walking, hearing and vision impairment, and acquired microcephaly. In some instances, children with HIV infection have normal neurologic findings, though this number is small. If the numbers of infected children reach predictions, HIV will become the leading infectious cause of mental retardation and developmental disability in children and will dramatically increase the numbers of children who will be in need of special educational and rehabilitative services. Because a HIV child's developmental pattern is apparently related to the encephalopathy, gains in motor and cognitive skills may be delayed from the early months, or there may be adequate progress at first and then a progressive loss of previously acquired skills. These children also show motor function abnormalities, with increased muscle tone, hyperreflexia, and altered performance. Language development commonly is delayed. These same phenomena may be caused by the presence of difficult child-rearing circumstances, other environmental factors, or the effects of chronic illness (Crocker & Cohen, 1990).

PROFILE OF THE NEEDS OF FAMILIES

A question often asked is, Who are the members of the HIV-positive child's family? Many times the mother has died and the child lives in a foster care home or a group home for babies born to infected mothers. This internal status of the family is of particular importance for the child's development, in that family needs are influenced by the family structure. Many of the mothers are products of economically depressed environments, poor nutrition, and diminished access or usage of prenatal care. At least 75% of these women are intravenous drug users, or sexual partners of men who use drugs. The single parent mother who is HIV positive needs medical follow-up, financial assistance, child care, respite care, and rehabilitation if using illicit substances. She also needs information about the course of her illness and what she can expect for the baby if he or she is HIV positive. She may need family planning counseling and information about safe sex practices.

A foster or adoptive mother will need information about AIDS and related illnesses. She will need information about handling body fluids of the infected child. She will need to be knowledgeable about the transmission of AIDS so that she can educate other persons who may have contact with the family. She may need information about early warning signs of illness and plans of action. She may need assistance acquiring information about support groups or individuals in her community. Most important of all she needs to know that it is natural to feel pain, anger, stress, and confusion, and that resources are available and accessible.

Families' needs are as diverse as families are different. Family needs may be in any or all of the following areas: education, health manage-

ment, health insurance, financial assistance, information seeking, and social and emotional support. Parents need training in language stimulation
techniques, nutrition guidelines, meal preparation, and financial and legal rights and responsibilities.

Given that the virus affects a greater number of African-American
and Hispanic individuals, it is important to address these groups specifically. Careful consideration and sensitivity to cultural issues is mandatory
in working with these families (Hopkins, Grosz, & Lieberman, 1990).

SERVICES AND RESOURCES

Interagency collaboration must be achieved among the medical and rehabilitation facilities, social services, legal and housing agencies, financing
channels, educational resources, and possible forces for advocacy. This is
a monumental yet necessary task. Mothers need drug rehabilitation programs that provide medical services and prenatal care for HIV-infected
mothers.

A number of professional associations have established guidelines
for providing services to individuals with HIV infection. An example is
the American Speech Language and Hearing Association which has pub-
lished a position paper on providing speech-language and hearing services to individuals with HIV infection.

Types of Services

Children with HIV infection require an array of services from many different practitioners. These professionals are employed in a variety of settings including hospitals, child development centers, clinics, and schools.
They have an important role in coordinating services and providing support. These professionals perform the following services:

- Screen and evaluate developmental progress, particularly during the
  first year of life
- Provide full assessments and recommendations for services needed
- Identify organic effects for HIV encephalopathy which requires spe-
  cial understandings when there is a background of deprivation
- Perform reassessments as indicated
- Monitor attendance problems due to medical reasons
- Serve as a child advocate
- Monitor the child's personal growth and developmental requirements
- Provide stimulation, training, and nurturing
- Make referrals to other agencies.

Education

In the case of P. L. 99-457, it is unresolved as to whether states will include HIV-positive status as fulfilling the "at risk" designation under Part H of that legislation, thereby warranting services (Harvey & Decker, 1989). Children with developmental disability as well as HIV, and children with congenital HIV who experience central nervous system dysfunction and developmental disability do fall within the scope of Part H of IDEA.

School-age children with HIV infection are entitled to free and appropriate education in least restrictive environments. As a result, schools have debated about attendance of children with HIV, including special education classes. Some of these children will not meet one of the definitions of handicaps under P. L. 94-142 during the early stages of their infection, but may qualify as the disease progresses.

Medical

Children with HIV infection do require medical management. They should be monitored medically on a regular basis and immunized on schedule as other children. These infants need to be tested for the HIV virus at birth and after the antibodies from the mother diminish at approximately 18 months of age. The babies who are truly infected begin to show significant levels of their own antibodies by that time.

Integration of Services

Integration of existing developmental services for children with HIV infections continues to be problematic in that they often have concurrent medical problems and live in circumstances of collapsed family support. For these children, the establishment of separate "specialized" day programs and residences has had some practical value, and much information is being gained about clinical and developmental supports in these settings. Confidentiality issues are more manageable in special programs, as well.

Barriers to Integration of Services

Several barriers exist that interfere with referring young children with congenital HIV infection to community-based developmental services. These barriers include:

- The developmental need has not been realized or identified
- The referral has not been made

- The family has overload, and does not wish an additional activity
- There is a local shortage of space, or logistical problems have not been resolved
- The receiving program has administrative problems
- Complicating medical problems predominate in the child's situation
- The effects of public opinion, at some level, are interfering.

NEEDS OF PROFESSIONALS

Primary care workers and program administrators who provide services for children with HIV infection have a demanding assignment laden with frustration and short on positive feedback. Practitioners providing services to this population have the following specific needs:

- Sufficient information to satisfy their intellectual curiosity
- To feel secure for their own safety
- To achieve agreement with the ethical issues
- To share in goal development and implementation
- To feel significant
- Opportunities to contribute new observations, ideas, and knowledge
- Sufficient training
- Opportunities for staff rap sessions
- Appreciation, including time breaks and visits to other programs to meet colleagues.

Developmental Model and Pediatric HIV Infection

Pediatric HIV infection poses a special challenge to professionals accustomed to working with children who are developmentally delayed. The developmental model views the child's condition as chronic and not specifically related to illness. Professionals thus focus on the child's progress or regression. In contrast, the parents of children with HIV infection focus on the child's illness, on the suffering that accompanies that illness, and on the inevitability of the child's death. When the caregiver is the child's mother who also is infected, these problems are compounded by the mother's medical condition and *her* fear of dying.

The contrast between the perspectives of professionals and families makes interaction between staff and parents of children with HIV infection especially difficult. The challenge for professionals in the field of developmental disabilities is to recognize and accept the different perspective that parents may have, and the potential for conflicting values held by parents and caregivers (Macklin, 1989). Children with HIV related diseases can develop disabilities that tend to be life-long. They can result in substantial limitations in the areas of self-care, receptive and expressive language, learning, mobility, self-direction, the capacity for independent living, and/or economic self-sufficiency.

CONCLUSION

The adverse effects of HIV infection on neurological functioning and development in children has been clearly established, and treatment approaches are changing to meet the needs of these diverse groups. As a result, the prognosis also is changing in terms of period of survival and rapidity of progression of the disease. Therefore, professionals who plan services for this population must consider these changes. Programs should be tailored to the individual's age and functional level, families' and caretakers' needs, developmental needs (i.e., communication, motor), and the medical and psychological factors characterizing the clinical course.

The availability of comprehensive medical and habilitative services for this newly emerging group of children who are developmentally disabled must be assured in the future. A coordinated effort among health, education, and other human service professionals must be available to provide the services required to address the complexities of HIV infection in children, and there must be open lines of communication between practitioners and families needing services.

REFERENCES

Anderson, P. P., & Fenichel, E. S. (1989). *Serving culturally diverse families of infants and toddlers with disabilities*, Washington, DC: National Center for Clinical Infant Programs.

Avery, B. Y. (1984). The status of black women's health. *Point of View*, Washington, DC: Congressional Black Caucus Foundation, Inc.

Belman, A. L., Diamond, G., Dickson, D., Horoupian, D., Llena, J., Langos, G., & Rubinstein, A. (1988). Pediatric acquired immunodeficiency syndrome: Neurological syndromes. *American Journal of Disordered Children, 142*, 29–35.

Bullough, V. L. & Bullough, L. B. (1982). *Health care for the other Americans.* New York: Appleton-Century-Crofts.

Centers for Disease Control. (1991). *AIDS Prevention guide for parents and other adults concerned about youth.* Washington, DC: U.S. Department of Health and Human Services, Public Health Services.

Cole, L., & Anderson, N. B. (1985). The economically disadvantaged. In L. Cole

(Ed.), *National colloquium on underserved populations*, Rockville, MD: American Speech-Language-Hearing Association.

Crocker, A. C., & Cohen, H. J. (1990). *Guidelines on developmental services for children and adults with HIV infection*. Silver Spring, MD: American Association of University Affiliated Programs.

Diamond, G. W., & Cohen, H. J. (1989). *Technical report HIV infection in children: Medical and neurological aspects*. Silver Spring, MD: American Association of University Affiliated Programs.

Dillard, J. M. (1983). *Multicultural counseling*, Chicago: Nelson-Hall.

Edmunds, P., Martinson, S. A., & Goldberg, P. F. (1990). *Demographics and cultural diversity in the 1990's*, Minneapolis: NES-TAS.

Frattali, C., & White, S. (1988). *Medicaid: Speech-language pathology and audiology service*. Rockville, MD: American Speech-Language-Hearing Association.

Guinan, M. E., & Hardy, A. (1987). Epidemiology of AIDS in women in the United States. *Journal of the American Medical Association 257*, 2039–2042.

Hanson, M. J., Lynch, E. W., & Wayman, K. I. (1990). Honoring the cultural diversity of families when gathering data. *Topics in Early Childhood Special Education 10*, 112–131.

Harvey, D. C., & Decker, C. (1989). *Technical report #2: HIV infection legal issues: An introduction for developmental services*. Silver Spring, MD: American Association of University Affiliated Programs.

Hopkins, K., Grosz, J., & Lieberman, A. (1990). Working with families and caregivers of children with HIV infection and developmental disability. *Technical Report*. Silver Spring, MD: American Association of University Affiliated Programs.

Jones, C. L., & Lopez, R. E. (1988). Direct and indirect effects on the infant of maternal drug abuse. A report for the National Institutes of Health/Department of Health and Human Services Expert Panel on Prenatal Care, Bethesda, MD.

Macklin, R. (1989). HIV infection in children: Some ethical conflicts. *Technical Report*. Silver Spring, MD: American Association of University Affiliated Programs.

Randall-David, E. (1989). *Strategies for working with culturally diverse communities and clients*. Washington, DC: Association for the Care of Children's Health.

Schilling, B., & Brannon, E. (1986). *Cross-cultural counseling*, Washington, DC: U.S. Department of Agriculture and U.S. Department of Health and Human Services.

Shelton, T. L., Jeppson, E. S., & Johnson, B. H. (1989). *Family-centered care for children with special health care needs*. Washington, DC: Association for the Care of Children's Health.

Sullivan, L. (1991). *Health care: Meeting the needs of the nation's poor. New Directions, 18* (2), 10–15.

White, S. C. (1990). *EPSDT—An improved Medicaid program*. Rockville, MD: American Speech-Language-Hearing-Association.

Chapter 4

Service Coordination Through Case Management

MICHAEL A. GILBERT
WILLIAM G. SCIARILLO
DEBORAH L. VON REMBOW

> The Committee intends that case management be an active, ongoing process of continuously seeking the appropriate services or situations to benefit the development of each infant or toddler being served for the duration of each child's eligibility. (House Report #99-860)

The above quote is from the "Report Accompanying The Education Of The Handicapped Act Amendments of 1986." This law amended the Individuals with Disabilities Education Act (P. L. 94-142) by adding Part H, which required the coordination of all resources and services to developmentally delayed infants and toddlers, and to their families. This legislation was significant because for the first time it required a single interpretation of the role for "case management" across the fields of health, education, and social services. It emphasized that only one staff person should be providing case management to a family at any given time. In defining "case management services" the government included

> Services provided to families of handicapped infants and toddlers to assist them in gaining access to early intervention services and other

services identified in the infant's or toddler's individualized family service plan; to ensure timely delivery of available services; and to coordinate the provision of early intervention services with other services. . . . (House Report #99-860)

FUNCTIONS AND ACTIVITIES OF THE CASE MANAGER

Case Management Services (in part) means:

> The activities carried out by a case manager to assist and enable a child eligible under this part and the child's family to receive the rights, procedural safeguards, and services that are authorized under the State's early intervention program. [34 Code of Federal Regulations, Part 303, Section 6]

Procedural safeguards encompass a number of different components to ensure the protection of family rights. The establishment of these safeguards is the responsibility of the State Lead Agency. The case manager is the person who informs the family of these procedural safeguards and assists them in using these procedures, as required by their needs.

It should be noted that during the reauthorization hearings of 1991, it was suggested the term "case management" should be changed to some other phrase such as "care coordination" or "service coordination." The term "case management" has been retained in this chapter to be consistent with the statute.

"Each child eligible under this part and the child's family must be provided with one case manager" [§303.6 (a)(2)]. The law requires that a case manager be only one person that the family works with, and that the person be responsible for:

Coordinating the performance of evaluations and assessments [§303.6(b)(1)]. This facet of the case management role presents a dilemma in that the case manager is identified as the person "from the profession most immediately relevant to the child's or family's needs" [§303.344(g)(1)], which may not be known until after the evaluation has been conducted. Therefore, some states have adopted the practice of assigning a person the role of "interim" case manager to fulfill the responsibilities of the case manager role until enough information is available to make a more relevant designation.

It is important to clarify what constitutes "evaluation" and "assessment" procedures. First, the purpose of *evaluation* is to determine a child's initial and continuing eligibility for early intervention services, and *assessment* is the process to identify a child's unique needs, and the strengths and needs of the family related to enhancing the development of the child. Assessment is the basis for establishing the extent and nature of the plan for early intervention services. This is not to say that the case manager is the evaluation expert in every domain of early development. It does say that the case manager is responsible to see that the evaluations are performed as required in the law. Assessment also needs to address the unique needs of the child in terms of different developmental areas and include the identification of services appropriate to meet those needs [§303.322(2)]. The five evaluation areas outlined in the law are:

Cognitive development
Physical development, including vision and hearing
Language and speech development
Psychosocial development
Self-help skills.

To facilitate the movement of the child and family through the evaluation and assessment processes, examples of specific case management tasks often include:

- Completing applications and consent procedures
- Obtaining copies of existing evaluation and assessment reports, including pertinent medical/health records
- Scheduling evaluations and assessments with consideration to the child and family's availability, including the child's sleep/wake and feeding schedules
- Assisting with transportation
- Supporting the family in being an active participant in the evaluation and assessment process
- Obtaining copies of completed reports from this process.

Facilitating and participating in the development, review, and evaluation of Individualized Family Service Plans [§303.6(b)(2)]. Each State participating in the Early Intervention Program for Infants and Toddlers (Part H) is required to develop a procedure to complete an Individualized Family Service Plan (IFSP) for every eligible infant, toddler, and their families. This procedure includes gathering information from the evaluation and assessment process and determining what services may be needed. There also must be a decision as to who will assume the ongoing case manager role. These considerations are intended to include input from the professionals involved in the evaluation, staff from agencies providing those indicated services, the family, and the interim case manager.

The ongoing case manager may be the interim case manager who was appointed at the time the child was initially referred and who has assisted the family through the evaluation and assessment and IFSP processes. Another alternative is that a new case manager more relevant to the child and family's needs may be indicated as a result of the evaluation and assessment processes.

The specific requirements of the IFSP process and document are found in the state regulations and administrative procedures of each state participating in the Early Intervention Program (Anderson, Place, Gallager, & Eckland, 1991). Specific responsibilities of the case manager may vary, depending on the needs of the family (Hurth, 1990). Sample activities throughout this process may include:

- Assisting the family in understanding the process and procedures, including their rights and responsibilities, relevant to the IFSP process
- Ensuring that an IFSP is developed within the 45-day period and that the plan includes input from the following:
  a. The parent(s) of the child and other family members requested by the parent(s)
  b. A case manager
  c. Person(s) directly involved in the evaluation or assessment process
  d. As appropriate, persons who will be providing early intervention services to the child or family
  e. An advocate or other person, as requested by the parent(s)
- Facilitating the active participation of the family in the IFSP process, including providing assistance, as needed in the following areas:
  a. Obtaining desired reports resulting from or related to the evaluation and assessment processes
  b. Scheduling of the IFSP and other related meetings, dependent on the family's availability
  c. Assisting with transportation
- Ensuring that the written IFSP is completed consistent with the established format, including:
  a. Medical and other services that the child needs but are not required under the early intervention program
  b. The name of the case manager who will be responsible for the implementation of the IFSP and coordination with other agencies and persons
  c. All indicated signatures
- Ensuring that a review of the IFSP is conducted every 6 months or more frequently if conditions warrant, or if the family requests it, to determine progress and whether modification of outcomes or services is necessary
- Ensuring that a formal IFSP review meeting is conducted on an annual basis
- Monitoring compliance with established timelines and other procedural safeguards
- Ensuring that all appropriate data is available for data collection.

Parents have the option of whether to sign the IFSP. They may choose not to sign if they wish to explore further service options or if they have any dispute with the contents of the plan. The 6 month periodic review may be held at a meeting or by another means that is acceptable to the parents and other participants.

Assisting families in identifying available service providers [§303.6(b)(3)]. Helping families to understand the maze of service providers has been a traditional role for the case manager in other service settings (Garland, Woodruff, & Buck, 1988). Typical responsibilities may include:

- Ensuring that the family receives information regarding the availability of service options (i.e., nature of services, eligibility requirements, location, hours, and so forth), including services needed that may not be entitled under the Early Intervention Program (e.g., non-covered medical/surgical services, and so forth).
- Supporting informed decision-making by the family in selecting service options.
- Assisting the family in negotiating with service providers regarding the services needed and related financial matters, including services that may not be covered under the Early Intervention Program.
- Assisting in the preparation of eligibility applications or insurance claims.
- Ensuring that the family is informed of their rights and responsibilities in regard to specific early intervention programs and services.

Coordinating and monitoring the delivery of available services [§303.6(b)(4)]. Keeping track of the service plan is a logical extension of the previous steps. Once needs have been determined and services identified, coordinating and monitoring the delivery of services may be of particular importance to a family receiving services from more than one provider. Responsibilities may include: maintaining ongoing communication with the family through home visits, office visits, telephone calls, and other follow-up activities; maintaining contact with, and facilitating communication among service providers, and between providers and the family; determining that services are being provided in a supportive and coordinated manner; assessing child and family progress toward identified outcomes; and assisting the family in monitoring the child's progress.

Informing families of the availability of advocacy services [§303.6(b)(5)]. The intent of this area of responsibility is to assist the family in understanding the general purpose and availability of advocacy services, including specific contact information, when less formal means of dispute resolution with the assistance of the case manager are not successful. The family members must understand their right to be accompanied and advised in administrative proceedings, including due process, by counsel, which may be provided by an advocate and/or by an individual with special knowledge or training with respect to early intervention services. Families may need clarification that the advocacy role of the case manager is not one of legal representation.

Coordinating with medical and health providers [§303.6(b)(6)]. Identifying medical and health needs in the IFSP does not impose an obligation to provide the services if they are otherwise not required as "early intervention services." Early intervention service providers must ensure that the IFSP contains a comprehensive picture of the child's needs, including the need for certain medical and health intervention that is not considered "early intervention services" (e.g., procedures that are surgical or purely medical in nature). The case manager needs to assist the family, as needed, in securing noncovered medical and health support. This assistance may be given by determining if there is a public agency (e.g., Medicaid, Early Periodic Screening, Diagnosis, and Treatment Program or the state Title V Program) that could provide financial and other assistance in helping the family seek out and arrange for their child to receive needed medical and health services.

In certain circumstances, such as a child who is medically fragile, it may be appropriate for the child's medical/health care coordinator to assume the role of case manager for early intervention services. Otherwise, the IFSP case manager should ensure the integration of the medical/health care coordinator into the planning process.

Facilitating the development of a transition plan to pre-school services, if appropriate [§303.6(b)(7)]. Many programs call for transition planning when moving from one type of service to another. On reaching the age of 36 months, toddlers are no longer eligible for "early intervention services" under Part H. Transitions are defined as points of change in services and in the personnel who coordinate and provide them. Times of transition often involve vulnerability and stress for children, families, and practitioners. Preparation for change should promote positive transition experiences and must be an integral part of initial and continuing planning for service delivery. The case manager needs to facilitate provision of steps to be taken to support the transition of the child on reaching age three to preschool services to the extent that those services are appropriate and/or to other child care, medical/health and social services that may be needed by the child and family.

The case manager needs to discuss with parents possible future placements and other matters related to the child's transition, including the financial aspects of services that will not be available after transition from Part H. There also may be the need to implement procedures to prepare the child for changes in service delivery, including steps to help the child adjust to and function in a new setting. The critical commodity at this stage is information that must be shared with the family.

Content of the Individualized Family Service Plan. The IFSP (see Chapter 1) must include the name of the case manager from the profession most immediately relevant to the child's or family's needs. This step will designate who will be responsible for the implementation of the IFSP and coordination with other agencies and persons. The "most appropriate person" also must fit the description "most immediately relevant to the child's or family's needs." This person, however, may not be the most acceptable to the family. In these situations, other alternatives must be sought. Any provider of services who may be integral to the needs of the child or family may assume the role of case manager. This decision will be made by the IFSP team, which includes the family. This selection may change as the needs of the child and the family change.

A MODEL OF CARE COORDINATION

The specific tasks of the case manager will change depending on the needs of the child and family and their particular abilities or desire to assume responsibility for certain tasks. It is predictable that the following events will happen more or less in sequence, but there may be considerable flexibility in individual instances.

Engagement

Building trust is the most basic function of establishing a relationship. Therefore, the purpose of "engaging" is to establish rapport with a family and to create a base to build a future relationship (Ballew & Mink, 1986). Clarifying and negotiating their expectations may not be significantly different from other settings, because the difference may be in the content of those expectations. The development and implementation of a service plan often will present a variety of challenges, both to the professional and to the family. It is important that the case manager and the family have a basis for communication in order to work together and solve problems.

Discovery

It is the stated intent of Part H that early intervention take a broad and holistic view of the needs of the child and the family. The stage defined as discovery includes the evaluation of the child in terms of eligibility for early intervention services and assessment of the child and family, in order to develop a plan. Assessment focuses on what developmental concerns are present, both in the opinion of the service providers and of the family, and what resources the family has to draw on to address those needs.

Because the IFSP is both a *document* and a continuous planning and review *process*, the case manager will participate, and facilitate the participation of others, in:

- Identifying the needs that the family and agencies would like to see addressed in the plan.
- Specifying the outcomes that will be addressed in the plan.
- Gaining agreement between the family and participating agencies on what outcomes will be specified in the plan and who will assume financial responsibility for each component.
- Developing an action plan to put the services into motion.
- Assigning, by mutual agreement among staff and family members, responsibility for components of the plan.
- Organizing and scheduling activities so the family can manage demands and agencies can plan staff availability.

Implementation

The implementation stage is where each agency follows through with their designated responsibility, according to the IFSP. The case manager monitors the plan to make sure services are provided according to the plan, and that the plan is appropriate and manageable on the part of the family. It may be necessary for the case manager to negotiate or advocate on behalf of the family to access or coordinate the delivery of services.

One of the guiding principles for case managers is to assume their role based on what the family will need or be willing to assume. In doing so, the case manager provides the family with the opportunity to meet the needs of the infant or toddler and be in control of the plan as much as possible.

Review

Review is an ongoing process rather than a single periodic event. It includes collecting information and monitoring the activity of the service intervention(s); measuring the activity against the expectations and outcomes of the IFSP; and re-evaluating the status of the plan, the progress being observed, and the immediate and long-term implications to the IFSP.

It is the responsibility of the service team to determine the merits of the service plan according to the timetable described in the IFSP. A review should take place at least every 6 months, and it is the responsibility of the case manager to see that the evaluation of the IFSP is done by those who are involved.

Disengagement

This phase is critical in that disengagement, that is, ending early intervention services to the child and family, needs to be a planned part of the IFSP process and not an abrupt ending or a "transfer" of the family to others. In many instances, there may be a predictable time when the case management relationship is no longer appropriate (Ballew & Mink, 1986). This instance could be when the child is no longer in need of active involvement, or is no longer eligible because of age. Disengagement needs to be well thought out so the family is well prepared to be in control of the situation after services end.

Disengaging procedures and planning may include other members of the service team, depending on the eligibility of the child for other program services. Depending on the services being provided to a child or family, those services may continue even though the child is no longer eligible under the title of "early intervention services," and planning needs to be made accordingly. Table 4-1 presents a summary of the events that occur as a part of case management.

THE PROVISION OF CASE MANAGEMENT

An aspect of the case manager role is the development of the ways in which staff will be available to families. This aspect creates a continuum of case management services and is described as a multilevel system of available resources that *may* include the following levels:

> Level I: *Families requesting peer support*
> In this situation, utilize trained parents or paraprofessionals.
> Level II: *Families needing a single service*
> Utilize a professional or paraprofessional from the most relevant service profession
> Level III: *Specific programs* (The State Title V Program, Single Parent Services, Protective Services)
> Utilize the case manager from the specific program in which the family is already engaged
> Level IV: *Multineeds families and multiagency services*
> Utilize a case manager from the arena of service providers that will fulfill the requirement that the case manager will be

Table 4–1 Case management in the early intervention system

Process	Product	Skills	Knowledge	Outlook
Engagement	Relationships established Expectations clarified	Listening Sharing complete information Advocacy	Local procedures Parent's rights Role as case manager	Family centered approach Resourcefulness Advocacy Inclusion rather than exclusion in EIS Risk taking Belief in change Leadership
Discovery	Statement of eligibility or ineligibility Identification of: • child outcomes • family concerns, resources, priorities • specific resources • agreement • action plan Complete IFSP document	Facilitating group process Collecting information Documenting Advocacy Linking Referring Negotiating	Eligibility requirements Child development Local procedures Confidentiality Parental consent Community resources Family dynamics	
Implementation	Services provided to child and family	Facilitating group process Collecting information Monitoring Referring Documenting Linking Assuming smallest role	Local procedures Advocacy Procedural safeguards	
Review	Continual review and affirmation of plan Periodic and annual formal review of IFSP	Facilitating group process Collecting information	Local procedures Advocacy Procedural safeguards Community resources	
Disengagement	Planned discontinuation of participation in EIS	Facilitating group process Linking Referring		

from the profession most immediately relevant to the child's or family's needs.

Included in a discussion on the continuum of case management is the issue of the "dedicated" or "independent" case manager versus the "integrated" case manager. A dedicated case manager is a person whose sole relationship with the family is that of case management. In this way, the case manager is not responsible for the provision of any other direct service and, conceptually, is in the best position to be an independent advocate on behalf of the child and family. Additionally, this gives that person the opportunity to become particularly skilled in understanding the early intervention system and in utilizing resources.

The "integrated" case manager is a person who is a direct service provider and a member of the group providing services to the family. The advantages of integrated case management are that the role is assumed by a person already involved with the family and, from a systems perspective, does not require the cost of adding a member to the group. On the negative side, this role requires that professionals assume a role that may be new and foreign to their experience and will require extensive training.

The continuum of case management, when viewed in this manner, offers a range of opportunities for the family and for agencies providing early intervention services. The ways case management will be available to the family will be decided by the State Lead Agency, which describes the early intervention program for the entire state. During the first 5 years of program development, a number of different tracks have been taken throughout the United States, and the variety of approaches will continue to evolve as each state implements the program.

Utilizing Existing Resources

When Congress funded Part H in 1986, it was thought to be adequate for statewide interagency planning and coordination of existing resources. The expectation was that these funds would be sufficient to assure the availability of comprehensive early intervention services, including case management, for eligible families.

The changing perceptions of a state like Maryland, from 1988 to 1991, is illustrative of experience with respect to providing case management. In Maryland, a survey of local public health, education, and social service agencies was undertaken to determine the current availability of early intervention services (Maryland Infants and Toddlers Program, 1989). Of 73 agencies surveyed (25 health departments, 24 local education agencies, and 24 social service agencies), 65 reported providing case management services using existing public funds. Thirty-one reported that their services were similar to those required under Part H, 27 claimed that their service could be modified without additional resources, and 15 agencies needed additional resources to meet the requirements. After several years of planning and initial implementation on October 1, 1990, more agencies reported the need for additional resources to meet the demand for case management services.

It has become increasingly evident that existing diverse case management activities occur in the context of a broad array of eligibility criteria and varying degrees of local and state discretion in establishing and selecting competing service priorities and populations served. In many cases, the case management offered could be described as system-centered rather than family centered. For example, the case manager determines eligibility for agency services, identifies needs as they relate to services provided by the agency, arranges for such services, and maintains records to fulfill the agency's reporting requirements.

As a part of the 1990 reporting requirements in Maryland, statewide interagency data were collected. In addition to the quantitative data, agencies were asked to identify at least three early intervention services in need of improvement (i.e, services not currently available; services in short supply; or services in a stage where further development is necessary). Case management was identified as the priority service in need of additional staff and training.

Although the comprehensive nature of case management under Part H may go beyond the historic experience of special education, the Individualized Education Program under the original Education of the Handicapped Act was intended to fulfill a coordinating function. More specifically, the concept of related services under Part B recognized that meeting the special education needs of children with developmental disabilities was more than a task for the education professional, requiring the coordination of the health and social service field as well.

Additionally, the legislative intent of many different sources of social service and developmental disabilities programs also include the comprehensive service needs, including case management, of individuals with developmental delay/disabilities or other vulnerabilities. For the most part, these are focused on specific eligible populations, many of which overlap with Part H, such as children under protective custody, in foster care, or with specific disabilities. It is difficult to generalize about such programs because they vary on a state and local basis.

In health care, the U. S. Maternal and Child Health Bureau has provided leadership toward a "family centered, community-based" interpretation of case management as an essential component of a comprehensive system of care for children with special health care needs, and their families. The Maternal and Child Health Services Block Grant Program, established under Title V of the Social Security Act, makes federal funding available to states for programs that are known as Children with Special Health Care Needs (CSHCN), as well as for other state maternal and child health care programs.

Pursuant to the Omnibus Budget Reconciliation Act (OBRA) of 1986 (P. L. 99-509) and 1989 (P. L. 101-239), a portion of Maternal and Child Health Services Block Grant funds to states were specifically earmarked for the development of community-based systems of services, and providing and promoting family centered and culturally competent care, including care coordination services. In accordance with this goal, the *Healthy People 2000: National Health Promotion and Disease Prevention Objectives Report* (U.S. Department of Health and Human Services, 1990) includes a system development objective for children with special health care needs. One objective, number 17.20, specifies the development of family centered, community-based, coordinated systems of services for children requiring interventions beyond routine care. Specifically addressed in the Title V statute are the service coordination needs of children under 16 years of age who are blind or disabled who receive Supplemental Security Income (SSI) benefits under Title XVI of the Social Security Act.

There is a great deal of variation among states' CSHCN Programs in the provision of care coordination services. This diversity is particularly found with respect to age and condition-specific populations served, and to the nature of the care coordination provided. At a glance, these services range from system-centered care coordination, best characterized as administrative case management, to family centered coordination efforts.

Perhaps the greatest opportunity available to states for supporting case management for early intervention is through the intersection of Medicaid (Title XIX) and the Maternal and Child Health Services Block Grant Program (Title V). The Title XIX statute requires that the state Medicaid plan describe cooperative arrangements with state health agencies to maximize coordination of medical assistance provided by those agencies. Title V also contains several statutory provisions for coordination with a state's Medicaid program because the programs have common populations, providers, and overall goals for child health.

An initiative in Maryland illustrates Title XIX-Title V collaborative arrangements which support case management in the early intervention setting. Since 1985, states have had the option under the Consolidated Omnibus Budget Reconciliation Act (COBRA '85, or P. L. 99-272) of providing as "medical assistance" case management services that assist Medicaid recipients to "gain access to needed medical, social, educational, and other services" (Association of Maternal and Child Health Programs, 1990). Unlike most Medicaid services, this service need not be available statewide or be available to all recipients in equal amount, duration, or scope. In other words, it can be "targeted" to certain subgroups such as children with disabilities. Because the case management services under Medicaid are similar to case management services under Part H, Maryland developed a targeted case management initiative for Medicaid/ Part H eligible infants and toddlers.

The Maryland Medicaid state plan amendment and the related state regulations, entitled "Early Intervention Services Case Management," identify the case management provider agency as the State Title V Program for Children with Special Health Care Needs (or Children's Medical Services) in conjunction with it's local health department designees. This arrangement will provide an array of qualified providers.

In most states there exists an array of case management resources that are complementary to Part H requirements. Funding streams that support activities to meet the comprehensiveness of these requirements are most readily identified for Medicaid-eligible children. It is meeting the needs for those children not eligible for Medicaid that presents the greatest challenge for states. This task will require going beyond existing resources and developing creative initiatives within the health, education, and social service communities. In view of the deteriorating fiscal condition in many states, this task will require a substantial increase in Part H federal appropriations and much creativity on the part of the states.

MAKING CASE MANAGEMENT WORK

As stated earlier in this chapter, case management under P. L. 99-457, Part H, is intended to be an active process that promotes family capacities and competencies, rather than promoting dependency or passive receipt of services. Consistent with other aspects of the statute's implementation, case management is to be family centered rather than agency centered. To say that effective communication is the key to successful case management is to understate the situation. A positive ongoing interactive process is essential.

The focus to this point has been to define and explain the required roles, functions, and responsibilities of the case manager in the development and implementation of the IFSP. Additional components to highlight are the underlying issues, skills, and attitudes that foster effective case management.

Issues for Agencies Providing Case Management

One issue concerning the role of case management is the comprehensive nature of the role as described in the federal regulations. Many professionals from a variety of specialties in the field of early intervention have remarked that case management may contain elements of what they have experienced in the past, but all together, they represent a range of activities and necessary skills that go beyond the experience of many.

A physical therapist may remark that his or her skills involve working with the child in a room on a mat, and while they have worked with the family in specific ways, they have not been required to be aware of other resources in the community to assist the family in identifying available service providers. A community health nurse may be well aware of community resources for a variety of needs, but may never have had such a clear responsibility to inform the family of parents' rights and procedural safeguards that may include other agencies. These professionals see some aspects of case management as different from their traditional role with the family.

Another issue surrounding the impact of case management responsibility on an agency is the time needed to train personnel. Properly done, training in the variety of skills implied by the execution of case management will be very time consuming and will require a good deal of training design. The design will need to account for different needs from the different professionals represented in the field. It could be quite frustrating for professionals to be put in a new role and not be supported with adequate training and the time needed to make the transition.

Issues for Case Managers

The ability to function in a linkage capacity is probably the most critical skill for a case manager (Johnson, McGonigel, & Kaufmann, 1988). As long as one member of an early intervention team has comprehensive knowledge of available resources in a community, and maintains that information in an accessible format, others designated as case managers can utilize that expertise.

Flexibility in approach is another essential skill for case managers. Not only is it important for case managers to be able to provide families with resource and service options, it is also imperative for them to modify their involvement as the family's level of involvement increases and decreases.

The ability to advocate effectively is important. Sometimes the needs of families are not addressed directly by public services. Then the role of the case manager takes on issues outside of the family. Further, case managers are responsible for helping families become self-sufficient by providing appropriate information.

Issues for Families

The degree of family involvement in the process of early intervention must be determined by the family, and it is subject to change. Families need to recognize and voice their needs regarding participation, particularly since needs are subject to change as family circumstances and perspectives alter.

Families' values and cultural diversity (see Chapter 3) may be reflected in the selection of resources and services to be included in the IFSP. Partnerships with professionals are fostered when families share information, ask questions, and express opinions.

REFERENCES

Anderson, K., Place, P., Gallager, J., & Eckland, J. (1991). *Status of states policies that affect families: Case management*. Chapel Hill, NC: Carolina Institute for Child and Family Policy.

Association of Maternal and Child Health Programs (1990). *MCH related programs: Legal handbook for program planners/Medicaid*. Washington, DC: The National Maternal and Child Health Clearinghouse.

Ballew, J. R., & Mink, G. (1986). *Case management in the human services*. Springfield, IL: Charles C. Thomas.

Garland C., Woodruff, G., & Buck, D. M. (1988). *Case management*. (Division of Early Childhood, White Paper), Reston, VA: Council for Exceptional Children.

Hurth, J.L., (1990). *A typology of case management models*. NC: National Early Childhood Technical Assistance System (NEC*TAS), University of North Carolina.

Johnson, B. H., McGonigel, M. J., & Kaufmann, R. K., (Eds.). (1988). *Guidelines and recommended practices for the individualized family service plan*. Washington, DC: Association for the Care of Children's Health/National Early Childhood *Technical Assistance System.

Maryland Infants and Toddlers Program (1989). *Survey of early intervention services, part 1: Local public services*. MD: Governor's Office for Children, Youth, and Families.

U.S. Department of Health and Human Services (1990). *Healthy people 2000: National health promotion & disease prevention objectives*. Washington, DC: DHHS Publication No. 91-50212.

Chapter 5

A Parent's Perspective: Empowering the Family

SUSAN N. HOCHBERG

Most parents anticipate the birth of a child with a great deal of hope and joyous expectations. Parents eagerly await their baby's first smile and first eye contact. They listen for cooing and babbling sounds and rejoice with each creeping or crawling movement. Their baby's first step and first words are sources of glee. Sadly, these perfect dreams are shattered when an infant or toddler has a condition or suffers an illness or accident that results in a developmental disability or serious health problem.

Acute pain, which accompanies the loss of this "perfect child" illusion, overwhelming feelings of disappointment, fear of the future, guilt, and anger are only a few of the emotions that families of children with special needs and developmental disabilities experience. These feelings have been unequivocally felt by this chapter's author, the mother of a child who is multiply handicapped and developmentally delayed, who at birth appeared to be that "perfect baby." Although the family lost their dream, in time they were able to replace it with realistic and fulfilling visions. As a family, they attributed their survival and success to a supportive network of involved grandparents, loyal friends, and Public Law 94-142, the Education of the Handicapped Act, which was passed by

Congress in 1975. This legislation enabled the author's daughter access to services through their local education system. Because P. L. 94-142 mandated that all children with handicaps were entitled to a free and appropriate education in the least restrictive environment, the parents were asked for input, to provide consent, and to be involved in the development of their child's Individualized Education Plan (IEP).

In many instances, P. L. 94-142 resulted in parents emerging as informed decision makers and active participants in their child's program. In "early infant stimulation" programs, combinations of home visitations and school-based interventions were utilized to provide speech and language therapy, occupational therapy, and specialized instruction. Often parents were trained in remediation and encouraged to implement those tasks at home. However, in spite of this legislative progress, the needs of the child within the context of the family were not specifically addressed.

During the ensuing decade, parents, educators, and legislators examined the critical role that families played, especially in the area of early intervention programs. In 1986, Congress amended P. L. 94-142 by enacting Public Law 99-457, including Part H the Infants and Toddlers with Handicaps, initiating a shift in focus from "child-centered" to "family centered" systems. The fundamental intent of this law was to "support families in meeting the special needs of their infants and toddlers with disabilities" [P. L. 99-457 § 671(a)].

PRINCIPLES UNDERLYING FAMILY CENTERED CARE

Empowering families requires changes in how systems deal with the emerging changes in the family structure, with nonmainstreamed lifestyles, with the occurrence of poverty, and with the increasing numbers of mothers in the work force. A family centered system is characterized by its flexibility in supporting and assisting families in their role as primary caregivers. It recognizes that the family is the center of the child's life and the "absolute constant." It views service providers as transitory, changing periodically as services change, while the family will remain (Silverstein, 1989). Family centered systems must reflect respect for differences in structures, values, and cultures (see Chapter 3), and recognize that families are independent and autonomous.

Families must be regarded as equal partners and need to understand how to cooperate and collaborate with professionals in all aspects of decision making. The resources, concerns, and priorities of the family and the choices they make are the driving forces behind the system.

OPERATIONALIZING CHANGES

It is often difficult to move from a child-centered perspective (P. L. 94-142) to a family centered focus (P. L. 99-457). Service providers, administrators, and systems personnel who historically were not involved with parents and families must restructure their thinking, philosophy, and orientation and include them in the development of their early intervention programs. Dunst, Trivette, and Deal (1988), suggest that change can occur through:

1. The adoption of a social systems perspective of families that suggests a new and expanded definition of intervention (Dunst, 1985; Dunst & Trivette (in press).
2. Movement beyond the child as the sole focus of intervention toward the family as the unit of intervention (Hobbs, 1975; Hobbs, Dokecki, Hoover-Dempsey, Moroney, Shayne, & Weeks, 1984).
3. A major emphasis on empowerment of families as the goal of intervention practices (Rappaport, 1981, 1987).
4. A proactive stance toward families that places major emphasis on promotion of growth-producing behavior rather than treatment of problems or prevention of negative outcomes (Dunst & Trivette, 1987).
5. A focus on family and not professionally identified needs and aspirations as the primary targets of the intervention (Dunst & Leet, 1987).
6. Major emphasis on identifying and building on family capabilities as a way of strengthening families (Hobbs, et al., 1984).
7. Major emphasis on strengthening the family's personal social network and utilizing this network as a primary source of support and resources for meeting needs (Gottlieb, 1983).
8. A shift and expansion in the roles professionals play in interactions with families and the ways in which these roles are performed (Slater & Wikler, 1986; Solomon, 1985; Trivette, Deal, & Dunst, 1986).

The value of family friendly, family centered early intervention programs must not be underestimated, because families have valuable and expert knowledge regarding their child. Combining these natural capabilities with the resources of skilled and experienced service providers will optimize the opportunity for the child's growth and development.

SUGGESTIONS FOR PROFESSIONALS

A family centered empowering approach will provide family members with the motivation for involvement, the opportunity for self-sufficiency, enhanced self-esteem, and hope. The following guidelines are useful for professionals who anticipate providing early intervention services.

1. Allow families to choose their degree of participation and involvement in the early intervention program. Their decisions are to be respected by professionals and service providers working within the system.
2. Consult the family when scheduling appointments and give options from which to choose. The time and location of planning meetings, diagnostic and evaluation appointments, and therapy sessions need to be convenient for the parents and family.
3. Maintain flexible hours that may include evenings and weekends. The increased number of single-parent households and mothers in the work force creates additional burdens and stresses. The hours between 9 A.M. and 5 P.M. Monday through Friday often are not feasible for families.
4. See that child care for siblings is available when required.
5. Arrange transportation if necessary. All families do not have access to public or private transportation.

It is important to remember that as children grow and develop, the needs and strengths of their families change. Therefore, family centered systems must be flexible, adaptable, and continuously responsive to these changes. Figure 5-1 offers a family support perspective that illustrates the changes that can affect a family.

Figure 5-1
Family Support Perspective

FAMILY SUPPORT PERSPECTIVE

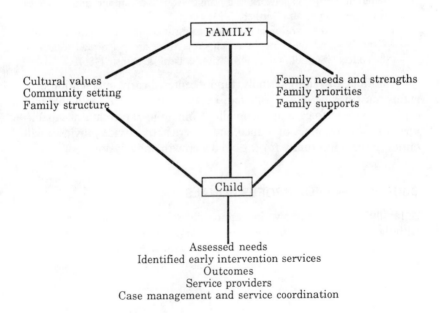

IDENTIFYING FAMILY CONCERNS AND RESOURCES

The Individualized Family Service Plan (IFSP) is the heart of Part H, detailing the early intervention services and the resources for the family. The sharing of information and the design and construction of the IFSP is predicated on the partnership and collaboration between family members and the professional team. The process of identifying the family resources and concerns must be confidential and should be governed by a respect for family privacy. At all times, it is important that the family feel it is an equal partner in the identification process, and that its unique views and observations are valued and respected.

There are many cultural styles, values, and alternative family structures in the United States. It is important for each family to define itself and to identify those individuals who have significant influence on their infant or toddler's life. Often the family composition may change, therefore the family also should have the opportunity to redefine itself accordingly.

The collaboration and partnership between parents and professionals should be ongoing and nonjudgmental. The identification of a family's resources and concerns is a continuing and evolving process, and because children and their families are very different, the extent to which they are willing and ready to participate in a collaborative process will vary widely. Early interventionists must be open-minded and flexible. The identification of a family's strengths and needs, and resources and concerns, must be based on the family's determination of what is most relevant in *their* lives, not what the professional perceives to be relevant.

THE VALUE OF PARENT SUPPORT SERVICES AND RESOURCES

Healthy People 2000: National Health Promotion and Disease Prevention Objectives (1990), reports that over the course of the 1990s the profile of the U.S. population will change. Based on the best available information, husband-wife households will decrease from 58 to 53%. Other studies suggest that within traditional two-parent households only 9% will claim nonworking mothers who remain at home as primary caregivers. These statistics, coupled with the facts that some single-parent households, children born and living in poverty, and children who are victims of abuse or neglect are increasing in numbers, pose unprecedented challenges to local and state systems. Nationwide, the viability of the family is threatened. Families of children with developmental delays and disabilities face long-term financial responsibilities and burdens that may threaten their survival. Because of increased levels of stress and anxiety, these families are also at higher risk for divorce or separation.

P. L. 99-457, Part H, ensures the availability of a coordinated, inter-agency, flexible, family centered early intervention system for infants and toddlers with developmental disabilities and for their families. At the same time, community-based parent support services, resources, and edu-cation programs are emerging throughout the United States. Many vary in approach and reflect unique community and available resources. Par-ent support services may be community-based drop-in centers that pro-vide parent skill and/or advocacy training along with child care (see Chapter 7). Other models may include recreational activities, emotional support, and socialization for children and their families. Family support programs are different from more traditional family services because of their emphasis on early and continuing support for parents. They view parents as partners in their program and not just individuals looking for service.

In essence, family support is based on a set of premises about par-ents, children, and what they need (Farrow, Grant, & Meltzer, 1990). When either an individual, organization, or agency is designing a parent, sibling, or family support program, the following concepts should be considered.

- All families need help at some time in their lives, but not all families need the same kind or intensity of support.
- A child's development is dependent on the strength of the parent-child relationship, as well as the stability of the relationship among the adults who care for and are responsible for the child.
- Most parents want to and are able to help their children grow into healthy and capable adults.
- Parents do not have fixed capacities and needs; like their children, they are developing areas of their lives, such as jobs, school, and other family and social relationships.
- Families are influenced by the cultural values and societal pressures in their communities. (Kagan, Powell, Weissbourd, & Ziegler, 1987).

It has been suggested that systems planners, professionals, and serv-ice providers adopt more flexible and sensitive philosophies toward fami-lies, if successful outreach to them is to be achieved. Farrow, Grant, and Meltzer (1990) suggest that effective supports and services for families should:

- Sustain and enrich the capacity of families to maintain a nurturing environment for their children. Rather than focus on deficits of the family, services should emphasize the existing strengths of families and help them supplement their own resources.
- Be available to families at the earliest stage of development and at subsequent stages, as needed, to strengthen coping capacities. Both

public and private resources could be organized to assist families and
their communities before they are confronted with an unmanageable
crisis.

- Rely on voluntary participation. Services should be developed and
provided within the context of a close, cooperative working partnership among families, their community, and program staff. The services should reflect the interests and cultural values of families and
link with other community resources that families already use.
- Provide parents with the skills and knowledge they need to advocate
for themselves and their children.
- Be multidisciplinary in approach and staffing to reflect a comprehensive approach to families' needs and situations.

Parents find solace, support, and acceptance of their children
through interactions with other families who face similar challenges. The
implementation of P. L. 99-457, Part H, the proliferation of parent support services, networking, and support groups ensures a brighter future
with greater opportunities for success among all children with disabilities
and their families.

INTERACTING WITH PROFESSIONALS

Current literature abounds with definitions and descriptions of the parent-professional partnership and its impact on early intervention. However, a very succinct but revealing analogy was offered by a parent of a
young child with developmental disabilities during a support group meeting. Depicting the future hurdles her child and family would face, she
alluded to the sports arena. She designated her daughter the "rookie
player"; she and her husband along with the professionals and service
providers constituted the team; the care coordinator assumed the role of
team manager. United, they established an equal and collaborative partnership that resulted in a victory that benefitted all.

This example of an effective parent-professional partnership is built
on mutual respect, trust, and nonjudgmental open communication. It
also stresses the belief that everyone must work together for a common
goal. Professionals are equipped with years of specialized training in targeted disciplines. Parents master months and/or years of intense observation and experience and become experts with regard to their children. The
ultimate challenge to systems is whether the diverse strengths, resources,
and visions of parents and professionals can be interwoven and integrated
for optimal service delivery.

SUMMARY

To provide *effective* early intervention services that will enhance the development of infants and toddlers with developmental delay and assist and support their families, the following principles must be incorporated in each service delivery system:

1. The philosophy of the early intervention system must be family centered and family friendly.
2. The provision of services must be flexible.
3. Parents or primary caregivers must be viewed as equal partners by service providers.
4. The identity and integrity of the family must be respected.
5. Parents or primary caregivers must be able to choose the degree of participation in all aspects of the early intervention system.
6. Parent and family support resources should be available.

Family life can be compared to a jigsaw puzzle that has many intricate pieces. A crisis occurs, and suddenly it is heaved into the air. When it lands on the floor, it is in total disarray. The challenge is to rearrange the pieces so that they will fit together and remain. One must realize however that families will rearrange their unique pieces with the different capacities, with unique styles, and in different time periods.

REFERENCES

Dunst, C. J. (1985). Rethinking early intervention. *Analysis and Intervention in Developmental Disabilities, 5*, 165–201.

Dunst, C. J., & Leet, H. E. (1987). Measuring the adequacy of resources in households with young children. *Child: Care, Health, and Development, 13*, 111–125.

Dunst, C. J., & Trivette, C. M. (1987). Enabling and empowering families: Conceptual and intervention issues. *School Psychology Review, 16* (4), 443–456.

Dunst, C. J., & Trivette, C. M. (in press). *Support Functions Scale: Reliability and Validity*. Unpublished scale, Family, Infant, and Preschool Program, Western Carolina Center, Morganton, NC.

Dunst, C. J., Trivette, C. M., & Deal, A. (1988). *Enabling and empowering families: Principles and guidelines for practice*. Cambridge, MA: Brookline Books.

Farrow, F., Grant, T., & Meltzer, J. (1990). Challenges and opportunities for public policies on family support and education. *Helping families grow strong: New directions in public policy*. Center for the Study of Social Policy, Family Resource Coalition, Harvard Family Research Project, and Maryland Friends of the Family.

Gottlieb, B. H. (1983). *Social support strategies: Guidelines for mental health practice*. Beverly Hills, CA: Sage.

Healthy people 2000: National health promotion and disease prevention objectives. (1990). (DHHS Publication No. (PHS) *91*-50213 1990). Washington, DC: Government Printing Office.

Hobbs, N. (1975). *The futures of children: Categories, labels, and their consequences.* San Francisco: Jossey Bass.

Hobbs, N., Dokecki, P. R., Hoover-Dempsey, K. V., Moroney, R. M., Shayne, M. W., & Weeks, K. H. (1984). *Strengthening families.* San Francisco: Jossey Bass.

Kagan, S. L., Powell, D. R., Weissbourd, B., & Ziegler, E. F. (1987). *America's family support programs: Perspectives and prospects.* New Haven, CT: Yale University Press.

Rappaport, J. (1981). In praise of paradox: A social policy of empowerment over prevention. *American Journal of Community Psychology, 9*, 1–15.

Rappaport, J. (1987). Terms of empowerment/exemplars of prevention: Toward a theory for community psychology. *American Journal of Community Psychology, 15*(2), 121–128.

Silverstein, R. (1989). *The intent and spirit of P. L. 99-457, A sourcebook.* Washington, DC: National Center for Clinical Infant Programs, Project Zero to Three, Grant #MCJ 113271.

Slater, M. A., & Wikler, L. (1986). "Normalized" family resources for families with a developmentally disabled child. *Social Work, 31*, 385–390.

Solomon, M. A. (1985). How do we really empower families? New strategies for social work practitioners. *Family Resource Coalition Report, 3*, 2–3.

Trivette, C. M., Deal, A., & Dunst, C. J. (1986). Family needs, sources of support, and professional roles: Critical elements of family systems assessment and intervention. *Diagnostique, 11*, 246–267.

Chapter 6

Preparing Practitioners for Early Intervention Services

JANEEN M. TAYLOR
DEBORAH L. VON REMBOW

According to Bailey, Simeonsson, Yoder, and Huntington (1990):

> Policymakers are faced with a significant dilemma of how to ensure that professionals providing services in early intervention programs are adequately prepared to do their work. (p. 26)

Part H of the Individuals With Disabilities Education Act (IDEA), Public Law (P. L.) 101-456 (U.S. Congress, 1990), contains provisions for 14 critical components of a statewide early intervention system. One, the *Comprehensive System of Personnel Development (CSPD)*, refers to initial preparation and ongoing education of early intervention service providers and parents. CSPD is a system encompassing several subsystems. These subsystems consist of:

a. preservice education
b. inservice education
c. continuing education and
d. technical assistance.

CSPD subsystems operate in a variety of settings, including community colleges, private and state colleges, universities, trade schools, state agencies, local agencies, private facilities, and other educational programs. CSPD and the subsystems contained within, offer important education and training opportunities designed to equip individuals with knowledge and skills critical to enhancement of infant and toddler development within a family context. In this chapter, CSPD and CSPD subsystems are examined.

Multiple avenues for initial preparation and ongoing education exist for a wide array of early intervention service providers. To acknowledge the variety of personnel involved with early intervention services, Fenichel and Eggbeer (1990a) suggest use of the term "practitioner." *Practitioners* are those who provide early intervention services. Early intervention practitioners can be parents, paraprofessionals, or professionals. CSPD addresses all phases and levels of practitioner preparation.

CSPD for early intervention is rooted in the foundation/youth legislation related to the education of children with disabilities, P. L. 94-142 (U.S. Congress, 1975), Part B. Part B contains provisions for a free appropriate education for students with disabilities. There is also a CSPD component in Part B, but it is designed primarily for personnel who provide special education and related services to school-age students. States must design and implement a CSPD for Part H and address the unique nature of infant and toddler development within a family context. Given the important philosophical and theoretical differences between Part H and Part B, there are a number of challenges associated with development of CSPD for statewide early intervention systems.

First, in Part B, there is a strong focus on "child centered services," and in Part H services must be "family centered." Part B federal funding is contingent upon development and implementation of an Individualized Education Plan (IEP). *Individualized Education Plans* are written evidence of planning relative to a free appropriate education in the least restrictive environment. Part H requires a different kind of documentation. The *Individualized Family Service Plan (IFSP)*, the hallmark of Part H, is formal recognition of the importance of families to child development in the earliest years.

Second, education agencies (federal, state, and local) have sole responsibility for ensuring a free appropriate education for all eligible children and youth of school age. This is described in Part B of IDEA and originally mandated through P. L. 94-142 which did not contain a mandate for services to infants and preschoolers. Early intervention and preschool special education were available at state discretion (see Figure 6-1).

Figure 6-1
Philosophical and theoretical
differences between Part B & Part H

Part B	Part H
IEPs	IFSPs
Single Agency Responsibility	Multiple Agency Responsibility
Smaller Multidisciplinary Teams	Larger Multidisciplinary Teams
Eligibility Criteria	Expanded Criteria

For example, in Maryland, a state law was passed in the late 1970s requiring a free appropriate education for all eligible children and youth *from birth* through the age of twenty. Local education agencies offered special education and related services, including programs for eligible infants and toddlers. A unidisciplinary model of responsibility for services to infants and toddlers resulted. While interagency collaboration was encouraged, responsibility for compliance was ultimately the responsibility of local and state education agencies.

Multiple agency accountability is required in Part H. The framers of Part H consider interagency collaboration and coordination critical to successful implementation of a statewide system of early intervention (Weiner & Koppleman, 1987). Several researchers conclude that interagency collaboration poses a significant challenge to full implementation of Part H (Gallagher, Trohanis, & Clifford, 1989; Meisels & Shonkoff, 1990).

Third, full implementation of multidisciplinary early intervention services, as required by Part H, necessitates a higher level of team cooperation than previously envisioned. Consistent with the educational nature of P. L. 94-142, Part B, teachers comprised the largest group of service providers (U.S. Department of Education, 1988) in the education of students with disabilities. With Part H, the list of potential practitioners is expanded. In addition to practitioners described in Part B, Part H includes

    a. psychologists
    b. counselors

    c. parent or family trainers
    d. health care practitioners and
    e. case managers.

Furthermore, the language of Part H is clear that *families must be considered key members of multidisciplinary teams*. Part H expands service parameters and increases the possible number of persons involved with early intervention. As a result, a greater degree of interpersonal and collaborative skills is needed (Garwood & Fewell, 1983) for orchestration of a wider range of resources.

Fourth, given the lack of accurate predictors of later developmental status (Gallagher & Ramey, 1987; Meisels & Shonkoff, 1990; Odum & Karnes, 1988), families and service providers are reluctant to assign young children to traditional diagnostic classifications related to eligibility determination. Terms such as mental retardation, specific learning disability, or severe emotional disturbance are inappropriate for children from birth to age three. In recognition of the malleability of early child development, Part H contains an alternative term, *developmental delay* (Smith, 1987), and has provisions for states to create a suitable definition. In many instances, definitions developed by states have extended eligibility for early intervention services to previously unserved young children and their families. Given census data, it is anticipated that increasing numbers of infants and toddlers with developmental delays (Brock, 1991) will enter statewide systems of early intervention as local projects move toward full implementation of Part H of IDEA.

CHALLENGES

As one component of a statewide system of early intervention, a CSPD must be developed to ensure that infants and toddlers with developmental delays and their families are served by qualified practitioners. Given the philosophical shifts from

    a. "child-centered" to "family centered" services
    b. "single agency" responsibility to "multiagency" responsibility
    c. "unidisciplinary" to "multidisciplinary" program models and
    d. expansion of definitional parameters,

several challenges have surfaced relative to full staffing of early intervention programs. One of the major challenges is *a severe shortage of personnel* (Dublinski, Weintraub, & Schipper, 1989; U.S. Department of Education, 1988) at a time when the "number of children served by special education and early intervention programs continue(s) to grow" (Staff, 1991). The problem of insufficient numbers of practitioners has been exacerbated by *high rates of staff turnover* (Palsha, Bailey, Vandiviere, & Munn, 1990; Palsha & Rennells, 1990). Early intervention program directors, anxious to fill vacancies, are forced to hire paraprofessionals and professionals who have generic licensure or certification, but lack knowledge and skills specifically related to infants, toddlers, and their families (McCollum & Bailey, 1991; Thorp & McCollum, 1988).

Another obstacle to full staffing of early intervention programs is lack of practitioner preparation programs with a specific focus on infancy (Bailey, 1989; Carriker, 1989; Yoder & Coleman, 1990). Basic programs leading to generic degrees in special education, nursing, nutrition, physical therapy, or other relevant occupations are not likely to include coursework or clinical experience related to infants, toddlers, or families (Fenichel & Eggbeer, 1990a). According to Bailey (1989):

> Work with handicapped infants...requires specialized (paraprofessional or) professional training because of the unique characteristics of children served, the complexity of the early intervention context, and the central role of families. (p. 107)

Shortages, staff turnover, and lack of specialized training are critical obstacles to full implementation of a statewide, comprehensive, coordinated, multidisciplinary, interagency program of early intervention services for infants and toddlers who are developmentally delayed and their families.

A COMPREHENSIVE SYSTEM OF PERSONNEL DEVELOPMENT (CSPD)

As described earlier, a CSPD refers to the statewide system of practitioner preparation and ongoing education or training required by Part H of IDEA. CSPD should be comprised of several *subsystems* that are linked and provide a full range of opportunities for initial and ongoing knowledge, acquisition, and skill training for early intervention practitioners.

Preservice Education

The first subsystem of CSPD is preservice practitioner preparation. Preservice educational activities are conducted at institutions of higher education, or post secondary programs. *Preservice education* involves pursuit of an accredited curriculum, leading to a degree or specialty certification. Graduates of a preservice program earn associate degrees, bachelor degrees, master degrees, doctoral degrees, professional degrees, or specialty certification or licensure. A sample of early intervention related fields that require degrees from a preservice program are special education, nursing, pediatrics, occupational therapy, physical therapy, nutrition, and psychology.

Ideally, preservice offerings should match personnel needs within the state. To do this, statewide personnel needs must be assessed regularly. If the quantity and focus of available preservice programs is inadequate, current and anticipated personnel needs cannot be accommodated. Changing or adding preservice programs for early intervention practitioners can be a lengthy and challenging process (Gallagher & Staples, 1990). To facilitate faculty efforts on behalf of early intervention, statewide needs for personnel must be clearly determined and disseminated in a timely fashion to appropriate institutions of higher education.

Further, preservice curricular requirements may not include acquisition of infant, toddler, and family skills and knowledge. Thorp and McCollum (1988) offer an ideal model (see Figure 6-2) of infancy specialization that incorporates discipline-specific knowledge and skills with those considered essential for early intervention services.

Several states, such as Wisconsin, address this challenge by offering statewide faculty training institutes and support of discipline-specific curriculum development. In Maryland, a Training Consortium for Higher Education has been established to link higher education programs on behalf of infants, toddlers, and families (Taylor, 1990). The consortium approach can offer a forum for collegial exchange through annual faculty development conferences, newsletters, preservice program needs assessments, and publication of annual early intervention preservice directories.

Inservice Education

A second subsystem for preparation of early intervention practitioners is *inservice education* of existing personnel. People who are currently employed in early intervention programs and agencies may have a basic degree, license, or certification, but may lack specific knowledge and skills relative to infants, toddlers, and their families. Bailey, Simeonsson, Yoder, and Huntington (1990) found:

> The typical student completing a preservice, entry-level program has received minimal preparation to work effectively with infants who are at risk or who have disabilities, or with their families. (p. 32)

Inservice education can provide multiple opportunities for specialized training (Winton, 1990).

As with preservice efforts, inservice activities must be carefully linked to practitioner and programmatic needs. Needs assessments targeted to early intervention practitioners and program administrators should be conducted on a regular basis and used for planning related to inservice

Figure 6-2
A model for conceptualizing training and licensure
of infant specialists from different disciplines.
From Thorp and McCollum (1988).
Used by permission of the authors.

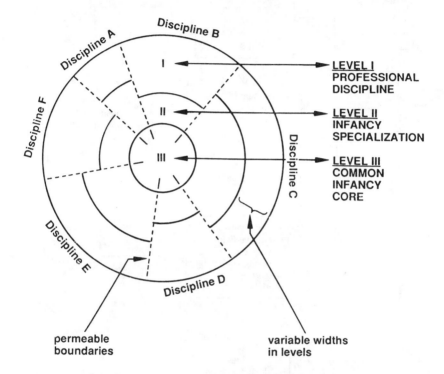

permeable
boundaries

variable widths
in levels

education. Typically, inservice education is offered on site and is tailored to specific program needs. Linder (1983) outlines a model (see Figure 6-3) for inservice education and provides a complete schema for linking practitioner education needs with a planned sequence of staff development and inservice education.

Continuing Education

The third subsystem of practitioner preparation is *continuing education* offered through professional organizations (Bailey, Palsha, & Huntington, 1990; Fenichel & Eggbeer, 1990b). Seminars and workshops sponsored by professional organizations provide a forum for members to acquire or expand their knowledge and skills within a specific discipline. New directions can be pursued for professional growth, or knowledge

Figure 6-3
A model for inservice education.
From Linder (1983).
Used by permission of the author.

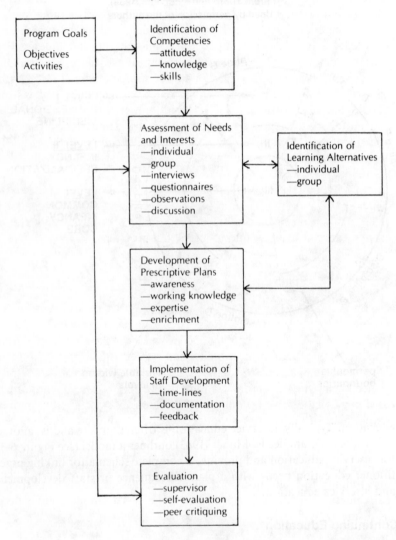

and skills can be updated for clinical application. Continuing education is essential for practitioners to "remain abreast of expanding knowledge in the field in order to perform competently according to current standards of practice" (Fenichel & Eggbeer, 1990b, p. 12).

Technical Assistance

A fourth subsystem of CSPD is technical assistance (McCollum & Bailey, 1991). *Technical assistance* involves matching resources to specific training needs. Resources may include technical experts, instructional media, written materials, or technology used in development of practitioner knowledge and skill. For example, Maryland's Infants and Toddlers Program has developed several important technical assistance vehicles. One, a *Lending Interdisciplinary Multi-Media Resource Center (LIMRC)* contains early intervention publications, reference materials, and instructional materials for use by early intervention parents, paraprofessionals, and professionals. Another technical assistance strategy involves development of an interagency *technical assistance team (TA Team)*. A TA Team is comprised of specialists representing appropriate social services disciplines.

In Virginia, there is an outstanding system of *technical assistance centers (TACs)* (M. D. Freund, personal communication, September 9, 1983). TACs offer materials, media, and trainers for purposes of technical assistance to local infant and preschool programs.

NEEDS ASSESSMENT

Garwood and Sheehan (1989) and Linder (1983) offer strategies for assessing practitioner needs relative to education and training. Data can be obtained from surveys of public and private providers, primary referral sources, parents, paraprofessionals, and professionals. In addition, reports from time-limited work groups, task forces, focus groups, and pilot projects, can further clarify training needs. Needs assessments can be used in a collaborative fashion to design interagency or interprogram inservice plans. Conducting inservice education, continuing education, and technical assistance in conjunction with other social services agencies, supports the multiagency intent of Part H of IDEA. Parents, paraprofessionals, and professionals should be offered a wide variety of education and training through an assortment of avenues to ensure high quality early intervention practitioners. Figure 6-4 offers a sample training needs assessment.

LINKING SUBSYSTEMS

CSPD subsystems must be linked to be effective. Bruder, Klosowski, and Daguio (1989) found a lack of coordination with regard to training between state agencies and other programs. With multiple disciplines, agen-

Figure 6-4
Training needs assessment

Based on your professional experience, please check 5 topic (s) you consider currently important to be addressed at a P.L. 99-457 conference:

_____ Screening	_____ Referral
_____ Child Assessment	_____ Family Assessment
_____ Outcome (Treatment) Planning	_____ IFSP (Individualized Family Service Plan)
_____ Transitioning Between Programs	_____ Facilitating Caretaker-Child Interactions
_____ Collecting Child Data	_____ Collecting Family Data
_____ Data Analysis	_____ Family Intervention
_____ Advocacy	_____ Teamwork
_____ Coordinating Services	_____ Communication
_____ Federal Laws and Regulations	_____ State Laws and Regulations
_____ Local Policy	_____ The Policy Process
_____ Program Efficacy	_____ Program Evaluation
_____ Procedural Safeguards	_____ Interagency Collaboration
_____ Program Funding	_____ Personnel Standards
_____ Dispute Resolution	_____ Care Coordination (Case Management)
_____ Legal Issues	_____ Communicable Diseases
_____ Professional Liability	_____ Environmental Modification
_____ Health Terminology	_____ Educational Terminology
_____ Supervision	_____ Goal Setting
_____ Time Management	_____ Lobbying
_____ Family Issues	_____ Conducting Research
_____ Multicultural Issues	_____ National Issues
_____ International Issues	_____ Child Care
_____ Respite	
_____ Other (please specify)	

_____
_____
_____
_____

cies, and programs involved with early intervention, cooperation and collaboration at all levels is essential.

Preservice training should relate to current and anticipated personnel needs as identified through state, local, and federal agencies. Inservice education should complement and expand on curricular offerings of preservice programs. Continuing education should address discipline specific skills and knowledge, yet facilitate interdisciplinary early intervention efforts. And finally, technical assistance should link resources to targeted training needs of individuals or programs. A well planned and executed CSPD (see Figure 6-5) supports practitioner preparation at all levels and is extremely important for high quality early intervention programs (McCollum & Thorp, 1988).

Figure 6-5
CSPD subsystems

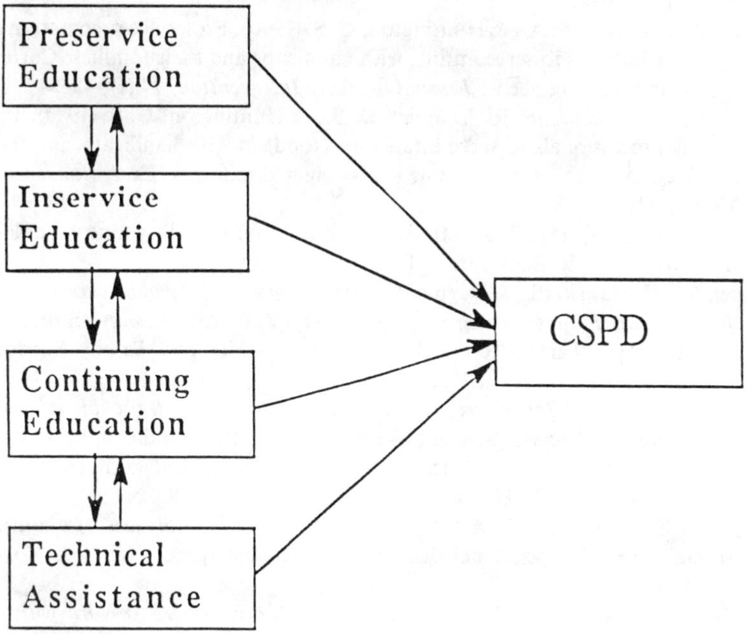

SUMMARY

A comprehensive system of personnel development (CSPD), one of the critical components of a statewide system of early intervention, is required by federal statute and regulation. States face an assortment of challenges and opportunities in the development of CSPDs. Specialized training is needed for quality early intervention services (Hanson, 1990). Preservice education, inservice education, continuing education, and technical assistance provide the principle subsystems of CSPD. The "long-term success of this (Part H) legislation ultimately will depend on the extent to which states can ensure that professionals working in early intervention are adequately prepared" (McCollum & Bailey, 1991, p. 57).

REFERENCES

Bailey, D. B. (1989). Issues and directions in preparing professionals to work with young handicapped children and their families. In J. J. Gallagher, P. L. Trohanis, & R. M. Clifford (Eds.). *Policy implementation and PL 99-457: Planning for young children with special needs* (pp. 97–132). Baltimore, MD: Paul H. Brookes.

Bailey, D. B., Palsha, S. A., & Huntington, G. S. (1990). Preservice preparation of special educators to serve infants with handicaps and their families: Current status and training needs. *Journal of Early Intervention, 14* (1), 43–54.

Bailey, D. B., Simeonsson, R. J., Yoder, D. E., & Huntington, G. S. (1990). Preparing professionals to serve infants and toddlers with handicaps and their families: An integrative analysis across eight disciplines. *Exceptional Children, 57*(1), 26–35.

Brock, J. (1991, May 15). Census finds biggest increase in Md.'s youngest, oldest. *The Sun*, pp. 1, 9. Baltimore, MD.

Bruder, M., Klosowski, S., & Daguio, C. (1989). *Personnel standards for ten professional disciplines serving children under PL 99-457: Results from a national survey.* Farmington, CT: Division of Child and Family Services, University of Connecticut Health Center.

Carriker, W. (1989). *A free appropriate education: But who will provide it?* Testimony presented to the Senate Subcommittee on the Handicapped and the House Subcommittee on Select Education regarding the Reauthorization of the Education for the Handicapped Act, Washington, DC.

Dublinski, S., Weintraub, F., & Schipper, B. (1989, May). Shortages of qualified special education personnel declared national emergency. *News & Notes*, pp. 1, 5.

Fenichel, E. S., & Eggbeer, L. (1990a). *Preparing practitioners to work with infants, toddlers and their families: Issues and recommendations for educators and trainers.* Arlington, VA: National Center for Clinical Infant Programs.

Fenichel, E. S., & Eggbeer, L. (1990b). *Preparing practitioners to work with infants, toddlers and their families: Issues and recommendations for the professions.* Arlington, VA: National Center for Clinical Infant Programs.

Gallagher, J. J., & Ramey, C. T. (1987). *The malleability of children.* Baltimore, MD: Paul H. Brookes.

Gallagher, J. J., & Staples, A. (1990). *Available and potential resources for personnel preparation: Dean's survey.* Chapel Hill, NC: Carolina Policy Studies Program, University of North Carolina.

Gallagher, J. J., Trohanis, P. L., & Clifford, R. M. (Eds.) (1989). *Policy implementation and PL 99-457: Planning for young children with special needs.* Baltimore, MD: Paul H. Brookes.

Garwood, S. G., & Fewell, R. R. (Eds.) (1983). *Educating handicapped infants: Issues in development and intervention.* Rockville, MD: Aspen.

Garwood, S. G., & Sheehan, R. (1989). *Designing a comprehensive early intervention system: The challenge of Public Law 99-457.* Austin, TX: PRO-ED.

Hanson, M. J. (1990). *Final report: California early intervention personnel model, personnel standards, and personnel preparation plan.* San Francisco, CA: San Francisco State University.

Linder, T. W. (1983). *Early childhood special education: Program development and administration.* Baltimore, MD: Paul H. Brookes.

McCollum, J. A., & Bailey, D. B. (1991). Developing comprehensive personnel systems: Issues and alternatives. *Journal of Early Intervention, 15* (1), 57–65.

McCollum, J. A., & Thorp, E. K. (1988). Training infant specialists: A look at the future. *Infants and Young Children, 1* (2), 55–65.

Meisels, S. J., & Shonkoff, J. P. (Eds.) (1990). *Handbook of early childhood intervention.* New York: Cambridge University Press.

Odum, S. L., & Karnes, M. B. (Eds.) (1988). *Early intervention for infants and children with handicaps: An empirical base.* Baltimore, MD: Paul H. Brookes.

Palsha, S. A., Bailey, D. B., Vandiviere, P., & Munn, P. (1990). A study of employee stability and turnover in home-based early intervention. *Journal of Early Intervention, 14* (4), 342–351.

Palsha, S. A., & Rennells, M. (1990). *Staffing early intervention programs: One state's status and future direction.* Chapel Hill, NC: Carolina Policy Studies Program, University of North Carolina.

Smith, B. J. (Ed.). (1987). *Position paper and recommendations of the Division for Early Childhood relating to P. L. 99-457 and other federal and state early childhood policies.* Reston, VA: Council for Exceptional Children.

Staff (1991, May 24). Special ed enrollment leaps, teachers scarce, OSEP says. *Education Daily*, pp. 1, 3.

Taylor, J. M. (Ed.). (1990). *1990 Directory of preservice programs.* Baltimore, MD: Maryland Infants and Toddler Program.

Thorp, E. K., & McCollum, J. A. (1988). Defining the infancy specialization in early childhood special education. In J. B. Jordan, J. J. Gallagher, P. L. Hutinger, & M. B. Karnes (Eds.). *Early childhood special education: Birth to three.* (pp. 147–162). Reston, VA: Council for Exceptional Children.

U.S. Congress. (1975). *Education of the handicapped act.* Washington, DC: Author.

U.S. Congress. (1990). *The individuals with disabilities education act.* Washington, DC: Author.

U.S. Department of Education. (1988). *Tenth annual report to Congress on implementation of the education of the handicapped act.* Washington, DC: Author.

Weiner, R., & Koppleman, J. (1987). *From birth to 5: Serving the youngest handicapped children.* Alexandria, VA: Capitol Publications.

Winton, P. J. (1990). A systematic approach for planning inservice training related to Public Law 99-457. *Infants and Young Children, 3* (1), 51–60.

Yoder, D. E., & Coleman, P. P. (1990). *Allied health personnel: Meeting the demands of Part H, Public Law 99-457.* Chapel Hill, NC: University of North Carolina.

Chapter 7

Implementing Early Intervention In A Child-Care Setting

CAROL ANN BAGLIN

Early intervention services include a variety of options that have traditionally been available, as well as certain family oriented support services. One of the most frequently requested services by families has been specialized child care that provides opportunities for parents to work and to participate in normal family activities with their other children. The problem, however, is the availability and appropriateness of these childcare services.

The factors that influence the development on infants and toddlers in child care revolves around the careful selection of settings and training of child-care providers. The context of the infant's experience of child care depends heavily on the relationship between the primary caregiver and the opportunity for the infant to form meaningful relationships during the course of a day (Pawl, 1990).

At a minimum, child-care programs must provide the infant and toddler with physical safety and protection. These programs also can function as a significant support system and source of basic information about child development for many parents. For the family with a young child with special needs, child care may also be the appropriate setting for early intervention services.

Child care providers who work with infants and toddlers often need additional special training and are the heart of quality programs (Daniel, 1990). This training includes learning to communicate in special ways with some children, as well as understanding the need for structure and the development of a supportive atmosphere. Particularly when providing care to young children with severe handicaps, child-care providers need special training in dealing with the unique behaviors of these children, such as responding to visual stimuli and postural orientation toward vocalizing (Rose, Calhoun, & Ladage, 1989).

The challenges of finding appropriate child care necessitate a basic understanding of how to identify the most appropriate child-care setting for the family, what to look for in finding quality child-care services, and how can child care be funded for each family as part of a comprehensive program, evolving in a setting that is most like that available to all children in this age range. For the family that wants or needs child care, the availability of child care for the infant or toddler with disabilities or specialized health care needs is dependent on training of personnel, supports to the provider, and information for the family and early intervention providers.

CHILD CARE AS A SETTING FOR EARLY INTERVENTION

Today, early intervention programs are being asked to look at families in new ways. This is a result of more mothers working, many young children growing up in single-parent families, and many single women having children at a younger age and with less prenatal care. The families of the 1990s need early intervention systems that are more accessible, more comprehensive, and more responsive and flexible. Other important options also will include implementing early intervention services in integrated settings, that is, settings in which infants and toddlers without disabilities would participate.

Child-care centers have increased from 18,300 in 1977 to 62,989 centers in the most recently available data (Pizzo, 1989) and many may be able to expand to encompass the delivery of early intervention services to infants and to include the family in the day-care setting. To date, child care as part of early intervention is viewed as having the potential to improve a child's performance upon entering school and to develop positive attitudes and self-concept. It also can promote greater consistency between attitudes and behavior among parents and siblings.

TYPES OF CHILD-CARE SETTINGS

Any mother returning to work or school following the birth of her child is filled with doubts about who is best able to care for the baby. Unfortunately, she often has few options from which to select. A mother with an infant with developmental problems or special health problems has the added problem of finding not only an appropriate facility, but unique caregivers with specialized skills. Some parents are fortunate in that they are able to have their parents or another relative provide child care. Others may be able to secure an in-home care provider such as a nanny or health aide. Many must rely on family day care or infant child-care centers.

Because specialized child care is in limited supply, parents must start the search for one early and rely on a great deal of luck, in many cases, to find the right provider. Parents can network with other mothers of infants with specialized needs and consult with local pediatricians for recommendations. Some larger urban settings offer Child Care Resource Directories that identify providers willing to care for children with specialized needs. Most child-care experts agree that it is the qualifications of the child-care providers and recommendations that are the best predictors of quality programs.

Family Day Care

Family child care is typically provided in a caregiver's home and is usually state or locally regulated. Minimally, regulations address health and safety standards. In some states, family day-care providers must register with the child-care licensing agency and are limited as to the number and ages of the children for whom care is provided. Family child care is usually less expensive than center-based care and offers flexibility in scheduling. The age groupings are frequently mixed and sometimes include school-age children for part of the day. There are an estimated 1.5 million family child-care homes in the United States. The average cost of care is $75 per week. Children under 5 years of age of employed mothers are cared for in their own home 31% of the time. This type of care is unregulated and frequently provided by relatives (Pizzo, 1989).

Many family child-care providers are themselves parents of young children. Frequently, parents seeking family child care mistakenly assume that parental experience ensures a good program and adequate knowledge of early childhood development (National Institute of Mental Health, 1978). However, a caregiver needs to have training in early childhood development and needs to possess the nurturing qualities necessary in caring for young children. With infants that have special needs, additional training and support is necessary to ensure an appropriate environment for child care.

Infant Centers

Center-based care for infants has been increasing in recent years due to economic pressures from many parents. Many employers require that mothers return to work immediately following release from their physicians. Until just recently, many states had not established regulations for infant center care, particularly when infants had developmental problems or special health care requirements. In the United States, only about 7% of infants and toddlers are cared for in centers, compared to 21% of this age group in France (Richardson & Marx, 1989).

Caring for infants in group settings increases many pressures and demands, especially those associated with diapering, feeding problems, sleeping, and dealing with individual infant temperaments. Centers providing child care for infants and toddlers should have separate areas for changing diapers, sleeping, feeding, and safe play areas. Because, the needs of infants and their families are specialized, programs must be willing to adapt to the uniqueness of each baby.

Parents should visit a prospective infant center during varied activities, such as meal time. During this time they can observe whether finger foods are encouraged, the method of bottle feeding, and whether meals are a pleasant experience for the children and adults. Adequate staffing also is important in centers with young children, and staff breaks need to be scheduled around mealtime, ensuring safety and enough adult hands during this process. Sleeping arrangements should include adequate ventilation, safety provisions, and cribs within view of adults who are supervising.

Cleanliness of the center is important to carefully monitor. Floors should be covered with carpeting that is easily cleaned and gentle on young skin. Food storage and cleaning of the diaper area are especially important in any center for groups of infants and young children. Creating the appropriate environment through physical layout enhances developmental motor activities and encourages physical movements, including crawling, running, and jumping. Young children need to be encouraged to explore and develop motor competence because this skill often helps to improve self-esteem.

Therapeutic Nurseries

Young children with specialized behavioral and emotional needs are sometimes placed in therapeutic nurseries for specialized care. These child-centered programs are characterized by a sensitivity to meeting the young child's emotional and developmental needs (Cataldo, 1984). The staff and settings of these facilities, besides meeting the needs of their children, frequently incorporate a family training component to support the family in their parenting skills. Staff ratios are usually lower between children and staff and must meet state standards in certification and licensing requirements.

Respite Care

Parents with young children with specialized physical and health care needs periodically need a break. Respite care provides these brief periods of time for parents to take a family vacation with other family members, or merely allow a parent to go shopping for several hours or take care of their own health needs. States may have respite care available through public agencies or may contract with private agencies to provide these services. Typically, sliding fee scales will be based on a family's ability to pay.

FUNDING

Comprehensive child care services for families are not available from a single funding source. Practitioners need to become familiar with the many programs that provide funding for services and frequently coordinate several to meet the varied needs of families. Current systems of financing are insufficient, but in combination with an early intervention program they can meet the full day needs of young children.

Purchase of Care

Many state child-care systems are overburdened and underfunded. Under the Title XX funds available to states, funding may be allocated to provide child care but only to low-income families. Under this arrangement, the state purchases child-care slots from providers for a specific number of children eligible under Title XX. The funds are provided to the child-care provider only for the specified period of time the child is to be in child care.

Employer-Supported Child Care

In many families, both parents work full time and as a result spend very little time with their children in their home. Increasingly, benefits that support the family are gaining in importance. Employer-supported child care for children is gaining in importance as a benefit for businesses seeking competent employees who will remain with the company. Inadequate and unreliable child care arrangements often result in lost wages and business, missed appointments, and vulnerable, unhappy children and employees. Almost half a million mothers lose time from work because of problems with their child-care arrangements, and working mothers spend about $11 billion annually on these child-care services (General Accounting Office, 1989). Companies are becoming sensitive to the link between employee satisfaction and meeting family needs, because corporations with on-site child care have lower absenteeism and turnover of employees.

Identifying Federal Funding Sources for Child Care

Comprehensive child-care programs for infants and toddlers can be supported through a combination of federal resources. These resources include several programs available under Title IV-A, for example, Child Care for Jobs and Education Training, Transitional Care, At-Risk Child Care, Child Care Licensing and Monitoring Improvement Grants. The Family Support Act of 1988 made child-care funds available to every child eligible for Aid to Dependent Children (AFDC). These funds are part of a larger effort to support AFDC families participating in employment or training. Under Title XX funds, states may provide child care to families with low incomes.

The Child Care and Development Block Grant provides states with federal funds to address affordability, accessibility, and quality of care. Under this legislation, states must use 75% of these block grant funds to help families pay for child care or to improve the quality of child care. Working parents are eligible for funding assistance if their children are younger than age 13 and their family income is less than 75% of the state median income. States are required to provide parents with certificates to help pay for the child care of their choice. Parents receiving these certificates may select any licensed, regulated, or registered provider. This care can include care by relatives, family child-care providers, religious institutions, and schools as long as these providers otherwise comply with state and local laws and the minimum requirements of the federal legislation. In addition, 25% of these Child Care and Development Block Grant funds must be targeted to early childhood education and children with special needs. These funds may be allocated through a public hearing process to develop unique approaches to providing child care to infants, toddlers, and their parents in specialized child-care settings.

REGULATIONS AND STANDARDS

The majority of children under 3 years old are in family child care. Yet most of this care is unregulated, not meeting even minimal health and safety standards. Up to 90% of family child-care homes are operating outside of the governing regulatory system (Corsini, Wisensale, & Caruso, 1988). Child-care centers in the United States do not have to comply with developmentally appropriate, or nationally recognized quality standards, and costs may be high, even though child-care workers are paid less on the average than parking-lot attendants (Broadwell, 1989).

Without utilizing regulated care some parents may identify excellent resources; however, some parents may place their children in a harmful situation. State licensing addresses the need for developmentally appropriate curriculums, qualified child-care providers, limits the numbers of children per caregiver, and sets minimum standards for health and safety.

In integrating early intervention services in the child-care setting, careful determination must be made that the child care provider is registered and meets the state's licensing and regulatory standards. This ensures formal training in early childhood development and can eliminate chronic turnover in personnel.

RESOURCES FOR SPECIAL NEEDS INFANTS AND TODDLERS

Information and Referrals

Parents seeking specialized child care can contact a variety of organizations and agencies to identify local providers. Child care resource and referral agencies can provide early childhood providers with information about specific state agencies or local providers. Child-care providers interested in providing specialized child care can contact their local or state agency responsible for implementing the federal legislation enacted under Part H of the Individuals with Disabilities Education Act (IDEA), the early intervention system for infants and toddlers with disabilities.

CHOOSING CHILD CARE

Availability

The child-care system in the United States is overwhelmed by the need for many parents to work and at the same time manage their parenting in a responsible manner. Half of the children under 1 year old have working mothers (Wilson, 1989). Some of these mothers are single parents with limited resources and limited choices. Availability of child care often is affected by the amount a parent can afford and where the child care is located. For example, working parents need to consider the distance from their employment to the child care provider in case their child may need them. Also, nursing mothers may want access to their young children during the day. Infants with special feeding or health care needs may require a parent to assist with these needs during the day. Parents with varied work schedules face special challenges in arranging for consistent and reliable child care for their infants.

Program Continuity During the Day

More than half of the infants and toddlers nationwide receive some form of regular child-care services, with nearly 25% being cared for in *two* or more arrangements, according to a report from the National Center for Health Statistics (1990). Continuity is important in planning for early intervention and day-long child care. At this time there are no reliable data on the use of child-care settings for early intervention; however, one study in New Mexico indicated that 40% of children served in early intervention programs were also receiving an average of 26 hours of child-care services (Sexton, 1989). In some communities, services for infants with developmental problems require parents to take their children to clinics or early intervention centers for brief periods for specific services. Because many parents are unable to take time from their jobs, or they have other children who must be cared for at home, early intervention services are not utilized.

Transition planning from early intervention services in a child-care setting to services in a preschool or nursery-school setting should take place early and involve the parents and staff as participants. Interagency coordination becomes increasingly important with the transfer of records and the need for continuity in the service plan. Transitions also may take place from home-based to center-based care and may include the introduction of new service providers for the infant and toddler. The passage of P. L. 99-457 formalized the need to address transition for the family as well as the child. The family's readiness for transition may be a factor that must be considered in the planning. Family services may now be provided through an alternative community setting and require independent follow through by the parents. Parents may need additional parent education and supports during this transition period.

Quality in Care Issues

Many parents want to know they have made the best choice in selecting appropriate child care for their child. Obviously providing for the health and safety of young children should be a priority in selecting a child-care provider. Young children requiring specialized and individualized care frequently need a coordinated program, integrating early intervention services into a setting of quality care. To achieve this, parents can be assisted in selecting a child-care setting by providing them with the information they need to make knowledgeable choices about a program (Howes, 1986).

To select a quality program, parents should make a list of all concerns and questions they consider to be important to their family. Next, they should set up appointments to visit the child-care homes or centers and observe the staff and the other children. It is important also for parents to meet with the staff and ask questions until they understand how the particular center operates in terms of their programmatic and developmental approach to infants, particularly children with specialized needs (Webster, 1990). Following is a suggested list of what to observe and what questions to ask.

Observe:

   Whether the children are content.
   The extent of staff involvement with the children.
   The cleanliness of the facility and the children.
   The use of restraints, such as gates, cribs, or tethers.
   Whether the children are being held and cuddled or whether they are in infant seats or playpens.
   Whether there is a high level of positive interaction and comments by the caregivers for individual children.

Question:

   Communication techniques between the child-care staff and the parent.
   Parent access to the facility.
   Discipline methods and use of corporal punishment.
   Health and safety issues: diapers, fire evacuation, emergency plan, refrigeration of foods and medicine.
   Who provides the food.
   Communicable disease policy.
   Payments, periods of lengthy illness, holiday breaks, family vacations.
   Use of substitutes during periods of absence for teachers and assistants and notification of staff changes.
   Staffing ratios.
   Certifications of teachers and training of support personnel.
   Availability of the licensing information and reports.

Follow-up on a visit can be done after the parent has had an opportunity to consider what has been observed and to formulate additional questions. Ask the child-care provider if you can talk with other parents who have children in the home or center. This step can help you better understand the issues you may wish to discuss. Parental access is an important component in evaluating child care. Some states have laws guaranteeing unlimited parental access. Parents are sometimes denied access by well meaning caregivers concerned that unannounced parents may disturb napping children or disrupt the routines. Parents should insist on unrestricted access to their child and should routinely drop by unannounced to determine the practices in the particular child-care setting.

SPECIAL ISSUES

Young children in child-care centers are more likely to require hospitalization than children in other settings (Centers for Disease Control, 1989). A review of children, age 3 and younger, in center care found that 5.7% needed to be hospitalized during a 6-month period. In addition, more cases of stomach illnesses and bronchitis are reported, but ear infections account for the largest number of hospitalizations. To minimize illness in group settings requires that parents and providers environmentally control illnesses through design of the facilities and sanitation procedures. However, due to the frequency of communicable diseases in young children, disease transmission is inevitable (Taylor & Taylor, 1989). Health care policies should be included in the child-care program's parent manual.

Another important step is to call the child-care licensing agency in the community and ask whether there have ever been any complaints about the facility or caregiver. Questions to ask include: What was the nature of the complaint? Was there an investigation, and what was the outcome? These reports, with the personalized information deleted, can be reviewed by the public, usually by appointment.

Awareness of child abuse and neglect are important issues for parents, providers, and early intervention personnel. The increased utilization of child care by parents requires they be aware of the risk of abuse but not unrealistically cautious in assessing child-care programs. Some states, but not all, have mechanisms for tracking individuals who have been convicted of child abuse, and this mechanism prevents their continuing to work in child-care settings. Child-care Licensing and Regulation Offices are required to investigate all allegations in child-care settings to substantiate complaints and when necessary require the provider to take corrective action. Many states are initiating training programs for child-care personnel that ensure an adequate supply of well trained providers for young children, decreasing the use of unlicensed care.

Parents have an important role in monitoring their child care arrangements through adequate visitation, routine inquiries of personnel concerning bruises or unusual physical complaints or problems, and involvement in all aspects of the child-care process. Preventive education can equip young children to resist the unwarranted use of authority and intimidation in child-care settings. Careful attention by parents in examining child-care policies that are aimed at preventing abuse can reassure parents about the relatively low risk of abuse in child care (Finkelhor, Williams, Burns, & Kalinowski, 1988).

Appendix A lists the major questions that should be asked before enrolling a child in a child-care setting. Parents are urged to discuss these questions with parents of children presently enrolled in the program.

INTEGRATED SETTINGS: DESCRIPTIONS AND UTILIZATIONS

Infants and toddlers with developmental problems, specialized health care needs or children with HIV virus or AIDS have a difficult time finding programs that will take them. As a result, child care may provide the most appropriate community-based setting for early intervention programs. Young children with developmental delays and specialized health care needs frequently can be provided with a full day of services, including early intervention and child care. These comprehensive programs can provide for educational interventions, therapeutic services, and parental involvement in a developmentally appropriate environment.

Itinerant Services by Specialized Personnel in the Child-Care Setting

Early intervention services can be provided during the day when the infant and toddler is participating in his full-day program. A report by the National Conference of State Legislators (1989) recommended that states look to child care and early childhood education as complementary, not competing programs. For infants and toddlers who are disabled, these programs can be implemented by qualified personnel visiting the child-care center for the specific purpose of delivering services that may be identified on an individualized family service plan (IFSP). These services usually are available on a fee-for-service basis through a private agency or individual, or can be provided as part of a caseload of a full-time public agency employee.

Early intervention Services in the Child-Care Setting

Young children with specialized needs frequently can be accommodated with supplemental early intervention services in centers providing regular infant and toddler care. For young children with developmental problems and their families, opportunities for informal interaction with infants without specialized needs can have a positive effect on development and parental attitudes. For example, both types of families need parent education, information about health care, transportation, employment issues, and the day-to-day stresses of modern life.

The child-care setting can facilitate the linking of quality services in a community-based location for families. Comprehensive service programs can be implemented through an array of prevention and treatment services in the familiar child-care environment. The combined location of staff and services from more than one agency can offer children and families the earliest access to comprehensive services (Melaville & Blank, 1991).

In designing child care that is developmentally appropriate for all participating infants and toddlers, there must be a commitment to individualized quality care. Meeting the diversity of needs of the children and their families in this type of setting depends on parental involvement, nurturing educators and child-care staff, and the availability of therapeutic interventions.

Trends in Staffing

Demands on staff concerning individualization and the requirement to meet the needs of all children in the child-care setting necessitate ongoing training and staff development activities. Developmental training regarding the physical domains of gross and fine motor, meeting the emotional needs of young children, varying the social activities, and stimulating cognitive development can facilitate diverse learning experiences. To meet the developmental needs of all young children in the child-care setting, the staff must be knowledgeable regarding typical physical development, psychosocial needs, and intellectual development. In addition, to enhance the planning process for individualizing the daily programming, an understanding of how a disability affects individual development is necessary (Newby, 1990).

Staff ratios of 1:3 with infants may support and influence planning and program implementation that can meet the daily needs of the staff and the children (Godwin & Schrag, 1988). With appropriate child-care personnel, the early intervention team can provide services that integrate a child into the child-care setting with minimum disruptions. Staff need to be provided with quality opportunities for interaction and assigned particular activities with infants.

To meet the specialized demands of providing care to groups of infants and toddlers, the Child Development Associate (CDA) Competency

Standards and assessment system for infant and toddler caregivers has been developed to provide standards for training, evaluation, and recognition of caregivers. A Child Development Associate is a person who has demonstrated specified competencies in caring for young children during an assessment conducted by the CDA National Credentialing Program (1987). The CDA is a national effort begun in 1971 to improve the competence of child-care providers and home visitors. The Competency Standards are divided into six competency goals which are statements of purpose for the caregivers that are common to all child-care settings. Functional areas are further delineated to describe the major tasks for the caregiver in order to complete the competency goal. Local Assessment Teams meet to collect information and to make decisions about awarding the credential. A CDA Credential is valid for 3 years from award and may be renewed.

First Start is another training initiative available through a licensing agreement with the University of Colorado. Developed at the University of Colorado Health Sciences Center, First Start is a 45-hour interdisciplinary course designed to prepare child-care workers and paraprofessionals to provide services for infants and toddlers who are handicapped or chronically ill. The program addresses all aspects of caregiving for children to increase the caregivers' sensitivity and competency with these infants and toddlers. Topics such as positioning and handling, feeding techniques, and care for children with a variety of disabilities and chronic health care problems are included, as well as opportunities to improve communication skills with colleagues and parents.

Curriculum and Materials

Working with the specialized needs of infants and toddlers with developmental problems involves the use of adaptive equipment and materials. Equipment not only supports motor development but can be designed to stimulate social interaction through its use by more than one child and mixed age groups. Adequate space is an important consideration in the design of play areas (Herbert-Jackson, O'Brien, Porterfield, & Risley, 1977). Convenience of access to materials and independence in selection can be facilitated through the location of materials and height of shelving.

An appropriate developmentally based curriculum should be provided for all young children in child-care settings that are designed to be more than custodial. In larger settings, grouping among infants and toddlers can be made according to mobility. As skills are acquired, younger children can be placed into older groups. Infants should be assigned to specific staff members to promote sensitivity in caregiving and continuity in programming. Charting of developmental tasks also should include information on each child's feeding and sleeping patterns.

Experiential approaches for young children are the basis for implementing developmental curriculums. Young children need to be encouraged to explore their environment through discovery of their own creativity and abilities.

SUMMARY

In a statement, the National Center for Clinical Infant Programs (NCCIP) agreed that:

> When parents have choices about selection and utilization of supplementary care for their infants and toddlers and have access to stable child care arrangements featuring skilled, sensitive and motivated caregivers, there is every reason to believe that both children and families can thrive. *(Family Support Bulletin*, 1988 p. 5).

This chapter has been about these choices and range of selections. The references that follow should be reviewed carefully for further detailed information. Also, state policy makers need to view child care and early intervention as complementary components of a supportive policy for families and important for their states. Communities are in the "hands-on" position to facilitate community-based solutions to providing integration in full-day settings for families. Will these changes take place thereby achieving the promise of P. L. 99-457? In jurisdictions with flexible providers, seeking creative solutions to competing demands and tight budgets, the answer, hopefully, is yes. It must be emphasized that it is to the benefit of all society to promote the inclusion of infants and toddlers with specialized needs in regular child-care settings. Everyone can grow through experiences that promote tolerance of individual differences, and all children benefit from an accepting and developmentally appropriate child-care environment.

REFERENCES

Broadwell, L. (1989, Fall). The complete guide child care. *Healthy Kids*, 27–32.

Cataldo, C. (1984, May/June). The child in child care. *Childhood Education*, 319–324.

Centers for Disease Control. (1989). Hospital infections program, Contact D. Bell, Atlanta, GA.

Corsini, D., Wisensale, S., & Caruso, G. A. (1988, September). Family day care: Systems issues and regulatory models. *Young Children*, 17–23.

Daniel, J. (1990, May). Child care: An endangered industry. *Young Children, 45* (4), 23–26.

Family Support Bulletin. (1988, Winter). *Consensus on infant/toddler day care reached by researchers at NCCIP: Family at the core* (p. 5).

Finkelhor, D., Williams, L. M., Burns, N., & Kalinowski, M. (1988). *Sexual abuse in day care: A national study.* Dunham, NH: Family Research Laboratory, University of New Hampshire.

General Accounting Office. (1989). *Child care selected bibliography.* Washington, DC: (GAO/HRD-89-98FS).

Godwin, A., & Schrag, L. (1988). *Setting up for infant care: Guidelines for centers and family day care homes.* Washington, DC: National Association for the Education of Young Children.

Herbert-Jackson, E., O'Brien, M., Porterfield, J., & Risley, T. (1977). *The infant center.* Austin, TX: PRO-ED.

Howes, C. (1986). *Keeping current in child care research an annotated bibliography.* Washington, DC: National Association for the Education of Young Children.

Melaville, A., & Blank, M. J. (1991). *What it takes: Structuring interagency partnerships to connect children and families with comprehensive services.* Washington, DC: Education and Human Services Consortium.

National Center for Health Statistics. (1990). *Child care arrangements: Health of our nation's children,* #187. Hyattsville, MD: U.S. Department of Health and Human Services.

National Conference of State Legislatures. (1989). *Child care and early childhood education policy: A legislator's guide.* Denver, CO.

National Credentialing Program. (1987). Infant/toddler caregivers in center-based programs, *Child development associate assessment system and competency standards.* Washington, DC: CDA National Credentialing Program.

National Institute of Mental Health. (1978). Parent-child program series, report No. 4, *Infant satellite nurseries: Family day care with a difference.* Rockville, MD: Center for Studies of Child and Family Mental Health.

Newby, P. (1990, Fall). Individualized child care for infants and toddlers. *Focus on Infancy, 3* (1), 1–3.

Pawl, J. H. (1990, February). Infants in day care: Reflections on experiences, expectations, and relationships. *Zero to Three, X* (3), 1–6.

Pizzo, P. (1989). *A tour of child care in the United States.* Washington, DC: National Center for Clinical Infant Programs.

Richardson, G., & Marx, E. (1989). *A welcome for every child.* Report of the Child Care Study Panel of the French-American Foundation, New York.

Rose, T. L., Calhoun, M. L., & Ladage, L. (1989, Summer). Helping young children respond to caregivers. *Teaching Exceptional Children.*

Sexton, D. (1989, Winter). P. L. 99-457: Implications for day and family care providers. *Focus on Infancy, 2* (2), 1–2.

Taylor, J. M., & Taylor, W. S. (1989). *Communicable disease and young children in group settings.* Boston, MA: College Hill-Press.

Webster, H. (1990, July). The best infant care. *Working Mother,* 8–70.

Wilson, L. (1989, Fall). Needed: Advocates for infants and toddlers. *Focus on Infancy, 2* (1), p 1–2.

Chapter 8

Managing Interagency Resources

CAROL ANN BAGLIN

In enacting P. L. 99-457, Part H, Early Intervention Programs for Infants and Toddlers, Congress recognized that young children with developmental problems and their families required comprehensive services that were unlikely to be fully available through any one public or private agency. Historically, services for young children developed largely as a reaction to specific needs and were crisis oriented, resulting in service systems that were not well planned or coordinated. Many states continue to report that coordination among their programs for children is difficult to implement (Harbin & Terry, 1991).

It is clear that state interagency efforts need to provide direction and leadership for the coordination of early intervention services. Policies and procedures need to facilitate community-based planning to provide a workable environment for practitioners and service providers. This may require a readjustment on the part of agency personnel in terms of specific service roles, job definitions, and the early intervention service delivery process. In this family centered legislation, parents also must have a greater role in negotiating the necessary services for their child and family.

Interagency coordination is both a process and an attitude. It is also an ongoing, active concept that can lead to solutions for some very complex problems. For example, professionals involved in interagency activities no longer may operate independently, but must progressively come together as a team. Coordination of multiple service systems can provide parents with the support and the coping skills that will allow them to access their own strengths, ultimately resulting in a higher quality of life for that family, as well as financial savings for everyone.

Outcomes of a coordinated early intervention system include a statewide organization of services for infants, toddlers, and their families. Using combinations of existing and specialized services, family outreach systems, and innovative funding patterns, gaps are filled in the service delivery system.

Nationally, the efforts to develop and implement P. L. 99-457, Part H, have resulted in the development of many community-based systems whose goal is to coordinate existing services and identify federal, state, and local initiatives. Traditionally, the early intervention system in each state is locally operated, within the federal and state requirements for implementation. Early intervention services include the variety of services that typically have been available, as well as certain family oriented support services such as respite care, specialized child care, and in-home aides.

HISTORIC TRENDS IN THE DELIVERY OF SERVICES

Professionals and families have long perceived the divisions that exist among the traditionally autonomous medical, human service, and education communities. These disciplines have maintained that their basic responsibilities to children with handicaps and developmental problems were separate and distinct. In reality, the services available over the last two decades through a wide variety of governmental programs for children and their families have blurred distinctions among these health, human service, and educational programs. Mandated services to children of all ages with special needs now transcend many of the historic boundaries of established service systems. Along with this attitudinal change, a broadening of perceptions of children and family needs has emerged (Magrab & Schmidt, 1980).

The major change in health services has been the new emphasis on preventing disease by promoting health in the family. These health initiatives have resulted from the coordinated efforts of the public agencies, the private sector, and individual professionals representing a wide variety of disciplines. Among the priority areas targeted for prevention activities are those directly related to consumers, such as pregnancy prevention, and prenatal and postnatal care for the infant, including immunizations.

The human service agencies have adapted their systems to incorporate the physical health and developmental status of children into planning for the psychosocial and economic well-being of the whole family. The emphasis in recent years has been on "wrap around" family support systems and interventions based on each family's identified needs and their individual family system.

There have been enormous pressures for increased services for children in the 1980s and 1990s. The 1970s were characterized by the development of equal access to services for individuals with handicaps and their families. The focus of education during this time has changed dramatically, particularly with the passage in 1975 of Public Law 94-142, The Education of All Handicapped Children Act. Under this law, all children who are handicapped are guaranteed a free, appropriate public education. Educational agencies were required to identify and evaluate children who were handicapped and to assure the provision of free and appropriate special education and related services. This move resulted in the expansion of health-related support services such as physical therapy and occupational therapy, not previously included in educational programs. Section 504 of the Rehabilitation Act (the "Civil Rights" law for the handicapped population) mandated comprehensive, nondiscriminatory services for individuals who were disabled.

During this same time, Title V of the Social Security Act provided key programs for children who were handicapped, Maternal and Child Health Services and Crippled Children's Services. The overall purposes of these programs were to: (1) reduce infant mortality, (2) improve the health of mothers and children, (3) reduce the incidence of handicapping conditions, (4) extend and improve medical and related services to children who were crippled, and (5) improve conditions of infants and children with handicaps.

With the consolidation of programs into block grants and dwindling resources due to budgetary and personnel cuts, the challenge in the 1980s and 1990s was for governments to provide coordinated, collaborative, and cost-effective services in the health, human service, and education areas.

A NEW EMPHASIS: THE FAMILY—THE PRIMARY CARE PROVIDER

The 1990s marked an approach where services for young children and their families was on treating the "whole" child. This focus reinforced the need for coordination, communication, and collaboration among a variety of disciplines to meet the needs of these young children who were disabled (Smith, 1988). Systems of comprehensive care today rely heavily on the family as the primary provider of services.

In 1982, important legislation known as the "Katie Beckett" Waiver, named after the first child to receive this waiver, recognized the importance of the family role in providing care to medically fragile children. It permitted states an option to provide for services at a lower medical cost in the home. Previously, these children would remain institutionalized because their return home would result in the loss of Supplemental Security Income (SSI) and Medicaid eligibility. In 1986, Congress enacted the Children's Justice Act which initiated temporary nonmedical child care in the form of respite services for families of children with disabling conditions or chronic illness. This Act prevented the unnecessary institutionalization and the permanent break up of the family system. On September 2, 1987, President Reagan signed Executive Order 12606 which ordered that the autonomy and rights of the family be considered by all departments and agencies in both the formulation and implementation of governmental policies. This order required that federal agencies recognize the role of the family as the primary force in the child's life.

HEALTH, HUMAN SERVICES, AND EDUCATION AGENCIES: SIMILAR GOALS, DIFFERENT APPROACHES

State and local agencies providing services for young children often share similar goals of providing cost-effective and efficient early intervention services. At the same time, however, it is necessary to recognize and understand their approaches and the uniqueness of these agencies. For example, each agency uses its own specialized language (acronyms), cites different legislative mandates, practices specialized intervention techniques, and develops staff training plans. The trend toward specialization has contributed significantly to the polarity among these service communities, often resulting in duplication and the creation of gaps in services (Hall, 1980).

Some of the different agency approaches are due to legislative mandates. For example, state and local education agencies have mandated free services for children who are handicapped, requiring the delivery of all necessary special education and related services, without regard to funding levels. Health agencies also may have legislative mandates (e.g., health departments are required to assist in school health programs), but generally have a more specific service orientation with finite budgets. Services may be paid for through private providers or clinic fees, income maintenance, or a targeted grant program. A variety of human services are made available according to specific age and disability, in combination with income eligibility. Eligibility criteria for health and human services can include age, disease diagnosis, financial need, geographic catchment area, and targeted areas of need. Eligibility criteria vary from program to program, and can be based on agency mandates, policies, state and local priorities, and limitations on resources.

There also are differences in the structure of services provided by health, human service and education agencies. State Departments of Education primarily provide management services, such as administration, monitoring, technical assistance, and fund distribution to local educational agencies (LEAs). State health and human service agencies frequently provide direct services through state-operated local agencies. These services may include medical evaluation and treatment, therapy, counseling, recreation, income maintenance, and a variety of support services to children and their families.

Education, health and human service agencies all may operate through a categorical approach to service delivery. That is, following some type of screening and diagnosis, specific probable services are indicated. Services by health and human service agencies often are provided based on income eligibility, certain court-related issues, or handicapping conditions with regulatory definitions that may differ from those utilized by educational agencies in implementing programs.

Young children and their families often need access to a variety of specialized early intervention services in their communities. Health, social services, and educational agencies, although they may provide many different avenues to obtain services, must examine methods for coordination through a single individualized family service plan (IFSP) (see Chapter 1). Although legislative mandates and agency structures may differ, common early intervention service goals among the programs can be identified and woven into a responsive early intervention system. It is important to note that health, social service, and educational programs for young children may be provided through the public or private sector, and may be state or locally funded.

Appendix B provides a list of the major services provided to young children and a sample list of what may constitute specific early intervention services.

Who Delivers the Service?

Young children with disabilities often have a variety of health, social service, and educational problems. Prior to the passage of P. L. 99-457, states

Figure 8-1
Early intervention IFSP direct services Part H
child-oriented services.

Child-Oriented Services

Special instruction
Speech pathology and audiology
Occupational therapy
Physical therapy
Psychological services
Case management services (provided to each child and
    family)
Medical services (for diagnosis or evaluation only)
Early identification, screening, and assessment
Health services (to enable child to benefit from other early
    intervention services)
Alternative living arrangements
Specialized day care
Transportation
Special Equipment
Health services
Nursing services
Recreation/adaptive PE
Nutrition services
Dental services
Specialized foster care
Immunizations
Assistive technology
Vision services

approached service delivery based on where the services originated. With the passage of legislative requirements for interagency service delivery, states have begun to examine methods for approaching system design across agencies and programs: (a) single agency only, (b) a dominant single agency coordinating services, (c) single agency in the leadership capacity, and (d) distinct separate interagency units (Harbin & Terry, 1991). Many states have been struggling with determining the most relevant profession to function as case managers (see Chapter 4), particularly when determining the responsibilities inherent in this role in acting on behalf of the lead agency and the family. Examples of child and family services that often are coordinated through case managers or "service coordinators" are listed in Figures 8-1 and 8-2.

Figure 8-2
Early intervention IFSP direct services Part H
family services.

Family Services
Identification of strengths and needs
Family training and counseling
Home visits
Respite care
Transportation
Homemaker service
Case management
Financial counseling
Protection and advocacy
Family education
Parent to parent networks and support
Interdisciplinary team services
Interpreters
Legal services

Generally programs focusing on young children stress early identification, screening, and evaluation. Most agency programs provide for individualized care or service plans, for example, Individualized Education Program (IEP), Individual Service Plan (ISP), Individualized Family Service Plan (IFSP), and Individual Treatment Plan (ITP). All of these plans contain similar structural features, such as evaluation information, specific interventions, and program planning. And, finally, agency programs usually provide some follow-up services.

Social service programs serve families with children and young people approaching parenthood. These programs provide emergency, crisis intervention, and assistance to families and individuals to increase their capacity for self-care and self-sufficiency. Also provided are intensive counseling on health-related problems, education, housing, training or employment, and family relationships.

THE INTERAGENCY PLAN: COORDINATION OF HEALTH, HUMAN SERVICE, AND EDUCATIONAL AGENCIES

Conceptualizing interagency coordination and collaboration has resulted in repeated attempts to clarify terminology and facilitate a sense of specific levels of success in approaching complex systems of service delivery (Intrilligator & Goldman, 1989).

The initial goal of the complex service delivery systems for infants and toddlers with disabilities is the coordination of efforts at the state and local level. Federal initiatives, including the development of joint policy agreements and model collaborative projects, represent a national commitment of time and resources to interagency cooperation. These federal incentives have helped to stimulate the development of active coordination of services at all levels.

The major goals of interagency collaboration are:

- To identify services and programs for infants and toddlers with disabilities.
- To promote awareness of specific agency and program mandates and responsibilities.
- To assure exchange of information and ideas among professionals.
- To facilitate coordinated service delivery on state and local levels through integration of services and policies.
- To maximize the use of existing resources.
- To reduce gaps and eliminate unnecessary duplication of services.
- To increase the cost-effectiveness of service delivery plans.
- To facilitate data collection efforts through interagency systems.
- To improve the effectiveness of family centered programs and early intervention services.
- To promote a core of quality services throughout the state.

To meet these interagency goals, health, human service, and education service providers are required to make a specific commitment to the team approach of working in family centered care (Intrilligator & Goldman, 1989; Magrab, Flynn, & Pelosi, 1985; McLaughlin & Covert, 1984). Service planners must work on the development and management of comprehensive service systems to ensure long-term coordinated approaches. Figure 8-3 presents the reader with an example of how the interagency system can function when everyone participates as part of a family centered team.

MAJOR POINTS OF INTERFACE FOR PROGRAMS SERVING INFANTS AND TODDLERS WITH DISABILITIES

Efforts to meet the comprehensive needs of infants and toddlers and their families involve the sharing of knowledge and meaningful coordination of services among disciplines. Many programs may retain a primarily educational, medical, or family emphasis, however, there will need to be a

Figure 8-3
Family centered interagency system.

INTERAGENCY SYSTEM

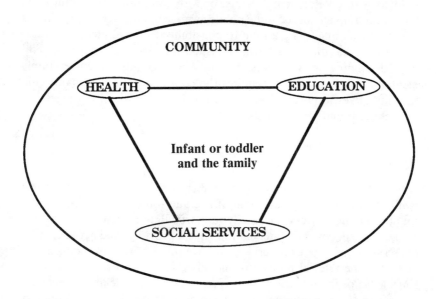

recognition of the value of the interdisciplinary approach in addressing the child in the context of the family.

Although many different services are provided by health, human service, and educational agencies, nearly all of these programs have some activities in common. Specific areas include prevention and early identification; referral; screening; eligibility determination; assessment, evaluation, and diagnosis; individualized family service plan; and service delivery.

Prevention and Early Identification

Health, human service providers, and educational agencies all focus on the early identification of conditions to prevent childhood disability and to reduce the long-term impact on families and society. The effectiveness of these efforts is measured in terms of the child's developmental status by improving the attainment of milestones, reducing the secondary impact of the disability, and assisting the family to function more effectively in response to their child's needs. The major disciplines with the relevant early intervention services and mandated responsibilities for the delivery of early intervention services are education and health.

All agencies involved in the location and identification of infants and toddlers with developmental delays, or with conditions that result in delay, do not implement the same public awareness outreach or procedures. State agencies may share a joint responsibility for child identification or may decide that one agency will be responsible for identification of children, depending on age ranges, disability, or eligibility categories. Implementation of P. L. 99-457 requires the coordination of all major child find initiatives to ensure the earliest possible identification of developmental needs and service delivery.

Referral

A thorough understanding of all available early intervention services will facilitate the process of referring infants and toddlers and their families for appropriate services and family supports. Referral resources must recognize the types of early intervention service providers and agencies, what the services are, where the services can be provided, who the contacts are, and what the referral process is, including coordination and follow-up. Knowledge of the referral process is essential to provide appropriate and responsive assistance to families. The referral process is a critical point of coordination in the service delivery system. This is the point at which the child and family are provided adequate information and supports, or is lost in the confusion of local and state bureaucracies.

Screening

Screening is the ongoing process of identifying children who present a likelihood of having special developmental needs. The purpose of screening is to obtain information about infants and toddlers to determine the need for a thorough assessment. An increasing number of medical, emotional, and social characteristics have been identified which indicate that a child may be "at risk" for developmental problems. Health, human service, and education personnel have placed increasing emphasis on providing these children with adequate early intervention services. Effective universal screening helps produce success in early intervention efforts. Coordination of interagency screening activities is significant in the development of any collaborative system of service delivery.

Screening processes can detect abnormalities in physical development, general health and vision, hearing, language, cognitive, motor, social, and emotional functions. Development of screening responsibilities, procedures for access to screening data results, and strategies for coordinating screening activities among local educational agencies, local health departments, primary care providers, and other providers are essential to ensure successful screening efforts. Identification of screening instruments, record keeping, data collection, tracking of screening results, parental and family involvement, utilization of community resources, follow-up, and continuity of services can be addressed through interagency procedures.

Eligibility Determination

It is difficult to overlook agency eligibility requirements for service. Many agencies have specific requirements such as nature of handicapping condition, age, financial eligibility, or geographical catchment area. These requirements are legislative mandates in some cases, agency policies in others. Service providers typically define their target client populations and structure their services to meet the needs of these populations.

Eligibility requirements therefore can interfere with the development of comprehensive service delivery systems. For example, a child may be eligible for services from one agency but not eligible for assistance from another. Sometimes families are lost in the variety of agency eligibility and regulatory requirements or these families may not meet any agency's target population. It is difficult to provide comprehensive services to a family without access to all the needed services and agencies.

Interagency coordination can be extremely useful in resolving problems resulting from varying eligibility requirements. Again, professionals in each agency need to communicate their roles and discuss perceived limitations in expertise, authority, and flexibility. With a clear understanding of who can provide which services for which client, professionals then can work on reducing any gaps in service to infants and toddlers and their families. Health, human service, and education agencies need to ensure the maximum use of existing limited service resources as well as consider alternative sources of assistance to meet the needs of families.

Assessment, Diagnosis, and Evaluation

Assessment is a systematic process of evaluation that measures an infant and toddler's physical, social or emotional status against established developmental standards. The result is a description of strengths and weaknesses, behavioral patterns, and level of functioning in a variety of developmental domains. Assessment provides information to document the impact of developmental delays and other conditions and supports recommendations for appropriate intervention. Assessment is both an educational and a medical term. The medical community goes through a similar process that results in a medical diagnosis. The diagnosis and description of conditions and medical functioning provide important information for planning appropriate services. The identification of family needs and strengths related to the infant and toddler's developmental needs is an important component in the implementation of P. L. 99-457, Part H. It necessitates a comprehensive approach to the family system and incorporates the development of the child as a significant factor in the functioning of the family.

Interagency and multidisciplinary evaluation of very young children who are suspected of having a developmental delay is critical. Local systems are required to pursue collaborative arrangements to identify potential developmental problems, to obtain assessment data results, to avoid duplication of testing among agencies, to develop procedures for tracking high-risk infants, and to coordinate a process for multiagency involvement in the determination of developmental delays. Interagency cooperation during the evaluation process helps ensure the accuracy of the diagnosis and assessment and promotes smooth transition to family centered program planning.

Individualized Family Service Plan

As explained more thoroughly in Chapter 1, individualized planning is a characteristic of health and human services, as well as educational services for children with special needs. An important issue among service providers and state agencies is the requirement of integrating various requirements into a single coordinated plan for young children. Federal agencies through targeted grants have encouraged health-related professionals and education professionals to use interdisciplinary team approaches to develop individualized plans. When more than one type of plan has been required, agencies were encouraged to develop a consolidated plan as long as it contained all required information and all necessary parties participate in its development. The individualized family service plan (IFSP) required under P. L. 99-457, Part H, focuses on a comprehensive approach to interagency developed goals and outcomes and on the method and criteria for provision of interagency early intervention service delivery.

The successful implementation of individualized plans depends partly on effective interagency and local and state agreements. These

agreements set the framework for implementation by describing the decision-making process for service coordination and implementation, and
by defining which services will be provided by health, social service professionals, and which services will be provided by educators.

Service Delivery

A wide variety of services to children and their families is provided by
health, human service, and education providers. Often, there is confusion
over which agency has primary responsibility for which services. Certain
responsibilities are unique to agency mandates or regulations and are not
usually duplicated, such as certain special educational services or specialized medical care. However, there is confusion in applicable federal and
state statutes for those services that might be provided by several agencies
to a young child and the family. Ideally, services should not be withheld
by one agency based on another agency having primary responsibility.
Still, agencies must determine which one will bear the cost of specific
services, which need to be justified in a specific agency budget, and which
exceed the statutory intent or budgetary limitations of that agency.

One of the ways agencies can determine the appropriate funding
source is through an interagency agreement, which should involve participants from the service delivery programs. In addition, other public and
private agencies that provide funds or services for young children and
families should be involved. In developing the agreement, a number of
criteria may be used to establish responsibility for financing services and
delivering the services in a coordinated and effective manner. The criteria
may include the geographical location of the service being delivered, the
qualifications of personnel furnishing the service, the financial eligibility
of the family, the overall purpose of the agency providing the service, the
period in which the service is provided, and the availability of personnel
and resources in the community. Deciding which agency provides personnel or funding for a given service depends on a careful assessment of state
and local factors and can be clarified through the process of interagency
coordination and collaboration (Zeller, 1980).

COORDINATION MECHANISMS

Interagency coordination is an ongoing and complex process in which all
levels of government need to be involved. In order to ensure long-term
collaborative approaches, formal arrangements should be made for interagency commitments, assignment of financial responsibilities, and service agreements. Although informal coordination activities have been

conducted among professionals in many communities, the lack of formal, written policies and procedures, can create problems in continuity of activities when the primary personnel important in the coordination process are no longer employed by their respective agencies. Turnover in personnel at the state and local level can also disrupt even the most successful coordination efforts, if those efforts have been based solely on informal interactions among existing personnel.

Administration And The Coordination Process

Interagency coordination and collaboration require time, patience, and communication at all levels. All professionals must carefully examine and reexamine their roles in this process and every effort must be made to facilitate, rather than hinder, the flow of services and information. As a first step, the parameters of the target populations must be defined, including the definition of the family. Also, agencies and programs serving the target population should be identified. The needs of the target populations, in this case infants and toddlers and their families, must be clearly delineated.

Next, the policies and service responsibilities of providers, especially those of identical or similar agencies or programs, need to be clarified. These programs then can be compared to identify duplications or gaps in services. Recommended program changes for improved collaboration and coordination then can be made. Because various funding options and constraints also must be determined, professionals need to be creative in the use of these funds and other available resources. It is important that different combinations and possibilities be considered.

The organization and authority for interagency decision making must be established. It may take the form of a council composed of consumers, local providers, and state agency representatives, or it may be a separate state authority or agency. In some instances, it could be principally an advisory group or board with decision-making powers.

Negotiating specific interagency agreements between service providers is a key step in the coordination process. Some programs that serve children with handicaps are required to develop cooperative agreements according to federal laws. The purpose of these agreements is to ensure that the services provided under state plans are coordinated with other public and private agencies providing services to children who are disabled. Also, efforts are made to use existing resources and to obtain appropriate financial support from other agencies.

Strategies for implementing program changes then should be determined. State and local planners need to decide the best techniques for bringing about change in the way that agencies and professionals relate to each other in the provision of services to the target population. A last step in the process, which should continue indefinitely, is to ensure the implementation of program changes at the service delivery level. This step includes state and local involvement in management, education, technical assistance, quality assurance, follow-up and program evaluation.

See Appendix C for the requirements for Interagency Agreements under the Part H system of early intervention.

Development Of Interagency Agreements

Written cooperative agreements are the foundation for most enduring coordination efforts among agencies. Such agreements provide a basis for professionals to begin working together, maximizing funds and resources (Elder, 1980). These agreements generally include:

- Overall and agency-specific goals and objectives of the agreement.
- Definitions of terms, specialized language, and jargon.
- Responsibilities of each agency and provider listed, including clarification of services provided at the state and local levels.
- Geographic catchment area of each agency and program.
- A system for referrals between agencies and transfer of records.
- Allocation of agency funds and resources.
- Uniform processes, forms, and standards for implementing similar programs by different agencies.
- A case management system and a system to ensure follow-up on services provided to the family.
- A mechanism to ensure continuing cooperation among agencies.
- The designation of staff who will be responsible for coordination activities at local and state levels.
- A system for sharing interagency information and data collection.
- Confidentiality assurances regarding sharing of information under differing regulatory systems.
- Specification of time period for the agreement.
- Periodic reviews of the agreement.
- Signatures of all parties responsible for implementation of the agreement.
- Evaluations of measurable outcomes at set intervals.

Types Of Agreements

Interagency agreements can include the following:

1. Establishment of common standards for similar programs. *Example*: Agreement between agencies and Early Periodic Screening Diagnosis

and Treatment (EPSDT) Program to establish specific criteria for identifying very young children suspected of having a condition in need of
assessment,

2. Allocation of agency resources for accomplishing mutual objectives. *Ex-*
    ample: Agreement between local agencies and a local hospital to estab-
    lish that the hospital will serve as the location for screening of NICU
    discharged eligible infants and toddlers,

3. Provision for maintaining uniform procedures, forms, and activities by
    agencies offering early intervention services. *Example*: Agreement be-
    tween child find personnel and community health nurses to use the same
    standard form for screening infants.

Commitment by key agency professionals is necessary to ensure the
effectiveness of interagency agreements. It is helpful to identify a person
from each agency to coordinate the development and implementation of
the agreement. The roles and responsibilities are defined clearly so that
coordination can continue if the designated person should leave the
agency.

In addition to identifying resources and services needed, agencies
should identify the benefits to each participant in the interagency process.
Professionals should monitor the effect of the agreement on services to
ensure that the outcomes are beneficial to the agencies and to the children
and their families. However, there are evaluation challenges for interagency coordination that are complicated by the complex nature of the
interagency effort (Magrab, Flynn, & Pelosi, 1985).

Individual Case Management And Monitoring Of
Services Provided

Coordination is also carried out through the management and monitoring of services provided to the family. The ongoing supervision of service
delivery enables health, human service, and education professionals to
work cooperatively to ensure that the most responsive services are provided to the families.

ISSUES IN INTERAGENCY COORDINATION

Interagency coordination often is a difficult process that must overcome
many long-term barriers. For example, the absence of effective professional and interagency coordination and collaboration can result in increased problems for families in obtaining services in their community. It
also can result in fewer referrals between programs and inadequate serv-

ices. These problems come at a time when families are least able to cope with additional stresses or unresponsive systems.

ISSUES IN INTERAGENCY PLANNING AND SERVICE DELIVERY

Negotiating agreements among multiple service providers frequently involves effectively resolving the following issues:

- Territoriality among agencies.
- Competition for funding between similar services and programs.
- Categorical programming for target populations in the family.
- Different approaches inherent in specialization.
- Absence of an integrated family centered approach to the family.
- Lack of communication among professionals.
- Lack of understanding of roles of other professionals or agency policies and procedures.
- Professional terminology and languages that accompany specialized knowledge.
- Agency policies and practices and program priorities.
- Differences in program eligibility requirements creating confusion and contributing to incomplete service plans.
- Agencies discouraging the need for additional intervention through another agency.
- Perceived threats to agency's autonomy.
- Increase in workloads for professionals.
- Varying agency priorities, mandates, and responsibilities.
- Conflicting organizational frameworks.
- Perceived confidentiality issues that limit information sharing.
- Narrow focus of agencies on the problem rather than the child or family.

Resolving these various issues (McLaughlin & Covert, 1984) can be handled through ongoing revision of interagency agreements or the development of broad areas of agreement with specific ongoing issues dealt with through policy management teams.

SHARING FINANCIAL RESOURCES: JOINT FUNDING OF EARLY INTERVENTION SERVICES

Interagency financing is an important component of effective and long-term interagency coordination. Knowing this, many state officials are concerned about the designation of certain agencies to pay for particular services. Although most of the major service programs are required to make use of all available sources of support, there is flexibility in the funding process.

One consideration in negotiating joint funding agreements is determining whether the resources of the participating agencies are adequate to pay for all required services. Some localities may have to develop collaborative agreements with additional resources to supplement agency budgets. Sometimes difficulties can be avoided through awareness of all major funding sources including health, human service, educational, other state and local, as well as public and private resources.

Since no one system works equally well in all communities, funding agreements may be in the form of generic agreements or individual agreements regarding a specific child and family. The generic agreement usually describes the specific population by age, target problems, or other factors, and specifies which services will be provided by which agency. The individual case agreement specifies which agency will pay for a given service to a particular child. State and local agencies must decide on the most appropriate form for their agreements based on local needs and available services.

Decisions on local funding for services should be based on the best interests of the family and the community, as well as the types of resources that are available. For example, professionals in a community with many private nonprofit agencies may want to involve these agencies in funding agreements and assure that they provide a share of the required services.

Additional considerations in joint funding include maximizing each source of funds to the state and community, maximizing services to the child and family, and distributing the cost of service provision equitably among all appropriate service agencies. These are key issues in a time of limited resources.

Impact of Block Grants

Legislative changes, shifts in priority services, and changes in funding levels have affected all levels of government. Some agencies have encountered problems in planning and implementing services during this changing fiscal climate. Often state and local officials have been faced with difficult decisions in the changeover from categorical to block grant funding, primarily because of the resulting reduction in federal funding. Regardless of the specific funding or priority services, it is crucial to have coordinated systems in place to ensure best use of limited resources. Coordination, cooperation, and communication must occur between and among levels of government. Meaningful interagency funding collaboration efforts are essential to improve service delivery to families.

One of the positive results of consolidation of programs into block grants has been the provision of more generic services: noncategorical funding allows for more comprehensive approaches, particularly with the varied and immediate needs of young children and their families. Interagency planning has become the most cost-effective approach to providing the continuum of services necessary for families whose members have specialized needs. However, since individual programs within a block grant may not be equally emphasized, the potential could exist for increased gaps in services for children. Service providers need to recognize and address these unmet needs.

IDENTIFYING FUNDING SOURCES

The planning and implementation efforts for early intervention services have gone forward with the dual purpose of both developing an effective program of early intervention services for infants and toddlers who are disabled and recognizing the fiscal realities of the late 1980s and early 1990s. Any initial attempt to estimate the economic impact of these services at state and local levels will have to incorporate the federal mandate that the early intervention services be a public-private partnership. Many eligible children already are receiving services in some form from public or private agencies. In many instances, these services are being provided in a vacuum, independent and unrelated to services being provided elsewhere. The true mandate of the Part H program is to provide for coordinated services, with both the service and financial responsibilities assigned to the appropriate agency. All of the early intervention services are being provided to the eligible child and his or her family in the attempt to prevent more extensive and costly services later in life. An effective program in the 1990s will produce savings in both institutional and out-of-state placement costs in the next century. It will further provide coordinated services to that group of the population that is most vulnerable.

The passage of P. L. 99-457 was based in part on the need to coordinate sixteen different federal programs that provide services for infants and toddlers with special needs (Smith, 1986). These programs, which are operated in several federal agencies, offer different services for different populations. See Appendix D for a listing of these programs.

IDENTIFYING THE GAPS IN THE EARLY INTERVENTION SYSTEM

Many eligible infants and toddlers and their families already are receiving early intervention services in some form from public or private agencies.

In many instances, prior to the implementation of P. L. 99-457, these services were being provided in a vacuum, independent and unrelated to services being provided elsewhere in the system.

Also, an analysis of identified funding sources in Part H, P. L. 99-457, Individuals with Disabilities Education Act, indicates that many of these do not directly provide services to infants and toddlers or may by State Plan Application limit the inclusion of infants in their service populations. In addition, not all of the funding sources are available equally to each state. Case management is essentially an unfunded requirement for each family and there are insufficient Part H dollars available to use for it. Few other programs provide case management services across the board to infants and toddlers and their families, although specially targeted case management through Medicaid is a possible resource for Medicaid-eligible families.

MANAGING THE AVAILABLE INFORMATION AND DATA COLLECTION SYSTEMS

Public Law 99-457, Part H, requires a statewide interagency system for gathering and maintaining demographic and case data about infants and toddlers identified as eligible for and receiving early intervention services. The cornerstone of these efforts evolves from the principle of early identification of potential difficulties and early preventative services to address the situation. This step will increase utilization of services early and ultimately should reduce the need for more extensive and expensive services at a later date.

Data collection is defined as the system for compiling data on the numbers of infants and toddlers who are disabled or at risk and their families in the state in need of early intervention services (EIS), the numbers of such infants and their families served, the types of services provided, and other information as required. In addition, this system would maintain the data necessary concerning the identified needs of infants and toddlers who are disabled and their families that could be used by the case manager to track assessments, interagency delivery of services, and appropriate transition planning at the age of three. The case management component is seen as an important role in this type of data system. In addition, a statewide central directory that includes early intervention services and resources is required to be developed and implemented.

> Within the statewide interagency system to be adopted by each State, Section 676 (b) (14) requires a system for compiling data on the numbers of disabled infants and toddlers and their families in the State in need of

appropriate early intervention services (which may be based on a sampling of data), the numbers of such infants and toddlers and their families served, the types of services provided (which may be based on a sampling of data), and other information required by the Secretary. (Public Law 99-457, October 8, 1986, 99th Congress)

The purpose of early identification of developmental problems of young children is to address their needs and the needs of their families by linkages to existing services. Additionally, it provides important aggregate data for reporting and planning purposes related to this population.

The goal of statewide early intervention systems is to foster the health and development of infants and toddlers with disabilities or those who are at risk of developmental delay, and their families, in order to:

- Facilitate early identification of infants and toddlers with or at risk of developmental delay and the delivery of appropriate prevention and early intervention services.
- Assist their parents to have access to and contact with services available to meet their needs, primarily through a tracking system and the case management model.
- Establish a statewide, interagency system of data collection for infants and toddlers to plan and improve services in a systematic way.

Any statewide tracking and data collection system for infants and toddlers and their families should be developed as an interdepartmental, integrated tracking and data collection system which, ideally, at the state and local level could be utilized to monitor program continuity and the provision of appropriate services to meet the needs of each child and his or her family. It is of critical importance to ensure consistent functions, terminology, and compatibility with existing systems to ensure the optimal level of interface. In the final analysis, both of these systems may best be operated at the local level as a component of a comprehensive interagency system, which will provide information for the state system, to be reported to the federal Department of Education.

Accessing The System

Although every agency requires agency-specific individual client information to facilitate the delivery of its unique services, all agencies need common and shared information if a comprehensive service delivery model is to be established. Therefore, it is critical to develop a mechanism by which an individual record for each eligible infant and toddler and his or her family is organized. This record is initiated at the time of the child's referral to the public system. It specifies those agencies that will provide services to the infant and toddler, providing the state lead agency with access to a single source aggregate of information to meet reporting requirements. This single interagency record allows for the tracking of a child among various service providers and eliminates the need for duplicative evaluations. The inability of states to resolve duplication problems prevents agencies from knowing whether children and families are being counted more than once for services (Hebbeler, 1991).

A centralized record mechanism for storage and retrieval of information can be limited to information an agency needs to coordinate service delivery and to fulfill reporting requirements. Initially, certain decisions need to be made to identify the data elements to be included in a record file to ensure that it can be accessible to each agency accessing the information. It can include:

- Unique identifier
- Service agencies
- Services provided
- Assessment information

Next, each agency needs to identify the significant issues in developing an interagency data system. This system includes:

- Input process
- Access
- Interagency confidentiality policies

Infants and toddlers and their families receiving services in an environment of shared resources and information are those who require the support and assistance from many public agency programs, including:

- Protective Services
- Intensive Family Services
- Foster Care
- Services to Families with Special Needs Children
- Respite Care
- Special Education
- Mental health, substance abuse, and developmental disabilities clinics and inpatient facilities
- Children's Medical Services
- Early Periodic Screening, Diagnosis and Treatment (EPSDT)
- Birth Defects

The following factors should be considered in predicting the validity of interagency data collection:

- Adjustments for duplication within and across agencies
- Analysis of expected annual intake per program

- Length of time a record remains open when a child no longer is receiving services from any program
- The impact of new service delivery systems, such as P. L. 99-457

Unique Identifier

An identifier for each child will be required because data will be added from a variety of programs and agencies, including the potential for several locations. Nationally, there are a number of states and program systems that have addressed the issue of establishing a unique identifier. The majority of these methods fall into the following categories:

1. Those generated by participating agencies from personal characteristics of the individual child such as the name and date of birth. This method enables all participating agencies to establish a number that is easily derived and which would be consistent among all service agencies.
2. Those created externally from the system, including social security numbers or birth certificate numbers. However, not every child has a social security number, the numbers are not frequently known, and numbers would need to be verified with the Social Security Administration.
3. Those created centrally and controlled centrally to assure uniqueness and validity. The system must be consistently maintained, updated, and enlarged.

The goal of an interagency data collection system is to improve services, encourage coordination, and reduce duplication through access to a centralized source of data on families being served or evaluated by any public agency or system. Data elements that describe information about the child that is not likely to change or need updating should be included to enable the system to match on a combination of fields. This step will help eliminate the duplication that results from even the most carefully constructed unique identifier.

INTERAGENCY COORDINATING COUNCIL

A major component of P. L. 99-457, Part H, is the requirement that each state appoint an Interagency Coordinating Council (ICC). This is a 15- to 25-member body required by the statute to be appointed by the governor in each state to advise and assist the State Lead Agency. The ICC has an important role in the coordination of resources and functions as a forum for public input in the development and implementation of the state coordinated interagency system of early intervention services. Parents of young children, pediatricians, advocates, public and private service providers, legislators, and state and local agencies have an important role in the development of a statewide community-based system of early intervention services. A typical mission statement is reflected in that of the Maryland Interagency Coordinating Council (Maryland Infants and Toddlers Program, 1988–1989):

> The focus of the Interagency Coordinating Council (ICC) is to ensure the provision of prevention and early intervention services which are coordinated, family-centered, and community based. ICC emphasis should be on supporting the role of the family, promoting interagency coordination, and anticipating interdisciplinary training efforts to ensure that personnel necessary to implement the early intervention system are adequately and appropriately prepared. (p. 2)

Many ICCs develop "guiding principles" to assist the members in formulating recommendations and providing assistance to the State Lead Agency. These principles frequently are cited in many of the state technical assistance materials developed by the national support organizations. Examples of these principles include the following:

- Parents are the primary decision makers regarding services for their infants or toddlers and themselves.
- Each "family" is able to define itself according to its own interpretation to encompass the primary nurturing caregivers and others who assume major, long-term roles in the infant and toddler's daily life.
- Each family is unique and reflects its own structure, roles, values, beliefs, and patterns. Respect for and acceptance of this diversity is a cornerstone of family centered early intervention.
- Early intervention must reflect a respect for the racial, ethnic, and cultural diversity of families.
- Early intervention services should be provided according to the normalization principle—that is, infants and toddlers and their families should have access to services provided in as normal a fashion and environment as possible and that promote integration of the child within their community.
- Early intervention programs should allow for individual community differences.
- Early intervention services should be implemented in a cost-effective manner through the integration and coordination of all available federal, state, local, and private resources.
- No one agency or discipline can meet the diverse and complex needs of infants and toddlers with special needs and their families. Therefore, a team approach to planning and implementing the IFSP is necessary.

State and local interagency coordinating councils have a major leadership role in effecting how influential the councils will be, and how much collaboration will be realized within states (Peterson, 1991).

COMMUNITY RESOURCES FOR EARLY INTERVENTION

A main purpose of Part H is to ensure planning and coordination of early intervention services for infants and toddlers, birth to age three, and their families. Accomplishing the promise of this legislation is dependent on the extent to which local jurisdictions can and are willing to develop their own capacity for coordinated and community-based service delivery systems. Agencies within any setting are competing for the same fixed resources, both dollar and human. There is a reluctance to support a new initiative that is perceived to be competing for the same resources. When this mandate emerges from an external agency, such as federal or state government, there also can be a reduced commitment to implement these collaborative efforts.

State interagency efforts need to provide direction for the coordination of early intervention services. Professionals are working to develop policies and procedures to facilitate community-based planning. Successful initiatives at the local level, however, will be the product of community activities that bring about the desired changes.

Interagency coordination is both a complex process and an emerging attitude. It is an ongoing, active concept that leads to collaborative solutions for some difficult problems. Professionals involved in interagency activities no longer operate independently but work together as a team. The overall result can be improved and less-costly services for children and their families.

A single coordinated point should provide for the entry to the interagency screening, a comprehensive evaluation and assessment, identification of the family needs and strengths, and the development of the individualized family service plan. Additional determination of family eligibility and access to interagency services could be facilitated, as well as the elimination of duplication in assessment and services. Further, Part H requires an extensive and continuous public awareness program. The public awareness program is the plan to advertise and promote, to both professionals and the general public, the single point of entry and the early intervention system, including how to make referrals and gain access to early intervention services.

CENTRAL DIRECTORY AND SPEAKERS BUREAU

Part H required the development of a central directory that contains a variety of data, including information about the availability of early intervention experts in the state. This directory of early intervention services needs to be readily available to parents, primary referral sources, early interventionists, and the general public. Gathering the necessary information will depend on the cooperation of the provider community and the ease with which data can be collected and collated in a logical format. Updating any directory will require many hours of work and continual contact with community resources throughout the state.

An additional part of any community-based plan to address the components of P. L. 99-457, may include establishing a Speaker's Bureau, which will:

- Reflect the statewide, interagency, multidisciplinary, family centered, and community-based orientation of early intervention, by including outstanding professional and paid professionals from a range of disciplines, parents, advocates, and legislators.
- Identify experts to address a wide variety of early intervention topics, including assessment, service delivery, family issues, personnel preparation, and legislative impact.
- Provide speakers, as requested, for state and local agencies, community organizations, business and professional organizations, and support or advocacy groups.

Surveys can be utilized to initiate the organization of the Speaker's Bureau and be disseminated to early intervention service providers throughout the community. This step will help to identify areas of expertise and develop a list of personnel willing to participate. A second survey can target early intervention consumers, as well as providers, to identify topics of interest. Data can be maintained to include names, titles, addresses, and telephone numbers of speakers, areas of expertise, and geographical areas speakers are willing to accommodate.

Each year an updated Speaker's Bureau Directory can be disseminated to all state and local agencies and public and private organizations responsible for the provision of early intervention services to infants and toddlers who are disabled or at risk and their families. Additional copies may be disseminated to parent support groups, advocacy groups, public libraries, and other information and sharing programs. Brochures and information kits pertaining to the availability and utilization of the Speaker's Bureau also could be developed and widely disseminated.

Communities vary greatly in their needs, resources, and approaches to service delivery. Agency mandates and responsibilities also differ. Although there is room for flexibility in interagency coordination activities, all approaches must be consistent with government policies and regulations and with local needs and resources.

INTERAGENCY COORDINATION: EVALUATING EFFECTIVENESS FOR THE FAMILY

Early intervention programs are being asked to look at families in a new way. The family is much different today than 10 years ago in that more mothers are working and many young children are growing up in single-parent families. Also, many single women are having children at a younger age and with less prenatal care. The families of the 1990s will need early intervention systems that are more accessible, more comprehensive, more responsive, and more flexible. Responsive services for these families can provide parents with the support and the coping skills they will need to effectively access a coordinated interagency system. Ultimately, this coordination will result in a financial and human savings and a service system that is supportive to families and reflective of the community.

REFERENCES

Elder, J. O. (1980). Writing interagency agreements. In J. O. Elder & P. R. Magrab (Eds.), *Coordinating services to handicapped children* (pp. 203–207). Baltimore, MD: Paul H. Brookes.

Hall, H.B. (1980). The intangible human factor. In J. O. Elder & P. R. Magrab (Eds.), *Coordinating services to handicapped children* (pp. 45–62). Baltimore, MD: Paul H. Brookes.

Harbin, G. L., & Terry, D. V. (1991). *Interagency service coordination: Initial findings from six states.* Chapel Hill, NC: Carolina Policy Studies Program.

Hebbeler, K. M. (1991). Creating a national database on early intervention services. *Journal of Early Intervention, 15* (1), 106–112.

Intrilligator, B. A., & Goldman, H. (1989). *The part H initiative: Towards a community-based service delivery system for infants and toddlers with handicaps and their families.* Arlington, VA: ICA.

Magrab, P., Flynn, C., & Pelosi, J. (1985). *Accessing interagency coordination through evaluation.* Chapel Hill, NC: University of North Carolina (Grant #GOO-84C-3515, START).

Magrab, P. R., & Schmidt, L. M. (1980). Interdisciplinary collaboration: In J. O. Elder & P. R. Magrab (Eds.). *Coordinating services to handicapped children* (pp. 13–23). Baltimore, MD: Paul H. Brookes.

Maryland Infants and Toddlers Program. (1988–1989). *Annual report year 2: October 1, 1988–September 30, 1989.* Baltimore, MD: Office for Children, Youth, and Families.

McLaughlin, J. A., & Covert, R. C. (1984). *Evaluating interagency collabora-tions*. Chapel Hill, NC: TADS, University of Chapel Hill.

Peterson, N. L. (1991). Interagency collaboration under part H: The key to com-prehensive, multidisciplinary, coordinated infant/toddler intervention serv-ices. *Journal of Early Intervention, 15* (1), 89–105.

Public Law 99-457. (1986). Amendments to the education of the handicapped act.

Smith, B. J. (1986). *A comparative analysis of selected federal programs serving young children*. Chapel Hill, NC: University of North Carolina (Grant #GOO-84C-3515, START).

Smith, B. (Ed.) (1988). *Mapping the future for children with special needs P. L. 99-457*. University Affiliated Programs, University of Iowa.

Zeller, R. W. (1980). Direction service: In J. O. Elder & P. R. Magrab (Eds.), *Coordinating services to handicapped children* (pp. 65–97). Baltimore, MD: Paul H. Brookes.

Appendix A

Selected Instruments for Assessing Parents and Families

SELECTED INSTRUMENTS FOR INCLUDING PARENTS IN THEIR CHILD'S ASSESSMENT

A Parent-Sensitive Model for Developmental Evaluation*
Assessment as Intervention: Discerning the Needs of High-Risk Infants and Their Families**

These checklists assist early intervention specialists with involving parents in their child's assessment by establishing a comfortable relationship, conveying clear information regarding the purpose and format of the evaluation, and incorporating information from parents about the child's behavior at home.

Source: Hanson, J. (1984*, 1988**). In J. Hanson & M. Freund. (1989). *A journey with parents and infants: Rethinking parent professional interactions.* Washington, DC: George Washington University.

The Family's Assessment Focus (Project Dakota)
Preassessment Planning: The Setting (Project Dakota)

The Family's Assessment Focus provides family members with an opportunity to share their observations about their child's behavior so that their concerns can be addressed during the assessment. *Preassessment Planning: The Setting* is a structured interview for parents to suggest their preferences for where and when to conduct the child's assessment. Parents also can provide suggestions for eliciting their child's best behavior.

Source: Kjerland, L., & Kovach, J. (1990). Family-staff collaboration for tailored infant assessment. In E. Gibbs & D. Teti (Eds.), *Interdisciplinary assessment of infants.* Baltimore, MD: Paul H. Brooks.

SELECTED INSTRUMENTS FOR IDENTIFYING FAMILY RESOURCES

Exercise: Social Support
This exercise presents four open-ended questions that can be answered in writing or orally. The questions focus family members on thinking about who provides their social support and what "roadblocks" may prevent them from accessing this support.

Source: Summers, J., Turnbull, A., & Brotherson, M. (1985). *Coping strategies for families with disabled children.*

Family Support Scale
This questionnaire assists families in identifying resources within their family, neighborhood, and community. Each resource can be assigned a rating on a five-point scale ranging from "not at all helpful" to "very helpful" with regard to raising children. Eighteen items include relatives, friends, co-workers, day-care center, and child's physician.

Source: Dunst, C., Jenkins, V., & Trivette, C. (1988). In C. Dunst, C. Trivette, & A. Deal (Eds.). (1988). *Enabling and empowering families: Principles and guidelines for practice.* Cambridge, MA: Brookline Books.

SELECTED INSTRUMENTS FOR IDENTIFYING FAMILY CONCERNS AND PRIORITIES

A "Snapshot" and the "Developing" Picture
This tool, a visualization exercise, is intended to help early intervention specialists and family members identify common goals or hidden concerns and judgments each may have related to a particular child. A written "snapshot" of a child engaged in a specific activity gives the team an opportunity to discuss how each member views the child. The "developing" picture, also written, is used to discuss how to facilitate desired developmental changes for the child.

Source: Developed by S. Kramer (1989) for Project Dakota Outreach, 680 O'Neill Drive, Eagan, MN 55121.

Family Needs Scale
This scale provides family members with an opportunity to identify in which of 41 different areas they would like some assistance. Each item can be rated on a five-point scale ranging from "not applicable" to "almost always." Items relate to daily childcare and family routines such as budgeting money, transportation, school placement, and having someone to talk to.

Source: Dunst, C., Cooper, C., Weeldreyer, J., Snyder, K., & Chase, J. (1988). In C. Dunst, C. Trivette, & A. Deal (Eds.). (1988). *Enabling and empowering families: Principles and guidelines for practice*. Cambridge, MA: Brookline Books.

Family Needs Survey, Revised

This survey gives families the opportunity to identify the topics they would like to discuss with early intervention staff. Six content areas are specified: information, family and social support, financial, explaining to others, child care, professional support and community services. The instrument consists of 35 items (and space for additional topics) which family members can rate on a three-point scale of "no," "not sure," and "yes."

Source: Developed by Bailey, D., & Simeonsson, R. (1990) at Frank Porter Graham Child Development Center, CB#8180, University of North Carolina, Chapel Hill, NC 27599.

Family Planning Questionnaire

This questionnaire provides family members with a format for identifying desired early intervention services and/or related information. It also provides an opportunity to communicate to early intervention staff their preferences for where and when to hold the initial meeting, as well as who to include.

Source: Developed by M. Dominguez, 1988, for Family Context Model, University of New Mexico, Albuquerque, NM 87131-5311.

How Can We Help?

This instrument consists of seven open-ended questions for family members to identify their concerns and priorities, followed by a checklist for identifying desired services in six areas. These areas include information, help with child care, community services, medical and dental care, talking about our child, and planning for the future. Each item can be marked by one of three choices: "we have enough," "we would like more," and "not sure."

Source: Child Development Resources, P.O. Box 299, Lightfoot, VA 23090.

Appendix B

Questions To Ask About A Child-Care Center

Licensing   Does the center or home have a license or registration?

Access   Is there full access during hours of operation? Does the facility have a drop-in policy for parents? Is there pressure to avoid certain periods of the day? Is there protection from indiscriminate public access?

Communication   How do parents contact the teacher? Are there regular parent meetings or parent training efforts? Is there a newsletter? How can the director be reached after hours of operation if there are concerns? Is the full name of the teacher provided and a regular means of contact available?

Methods of discipline   How are children disciplined? Under what circumstances is corporal punishment used? When there are problems are parents promptly notified?

Health and safety issues   Is there a method to monitor access to the center by the general public and delivery persons? Are the bathroom facilities visible and carefully monitored by two or more adults? Are children supervised at all times? How do children use the bathroom facilities during outdoor play? Are there policies for the care of ill children? Does the facility have a pediatrician available for emergencies? Are all accidents reported in writing to the parents?

Staff-child ratio   Is there sufficient staff to not only meet state standards but provide interactive relationships with the children? Are children grouped with appropriately qualified staff?

Nutrition   Who provides the food? Are there snack periods? How many adults are available to assist with feeding the infants? Are there high chairs available for infants that are safe and clean? Is self-feeding an option for toddlers? If the child has feeding difficulties, are their adults trained in specialized feeding techniques? Is food consumption reported to the parent, particularly for infants?

Staff policies   Are the staff certified? Are there ongoing training opportunities for staff in early childhood development? What is the staff-child ratio? What are the policies on substitutes? Are parents notified about staff changes? Have there been criminal background checks on all staff, including kitchen and custodial?

Field trips   Do children go on field trips? Are vehicles equipped with child safety restraints? Are parents always notified when children are removed from the site? If the family child-care provider transports children to other programs, who supervises the remaining children?

Costs   Are costs available in written material? What are the policies concerning holidays and sick days? What about long-term illness or family vacations? Are there sliding fee scales?

Outdoor activities   Is there a safe outdoor play area? Is there always supervision during outdoor activities? What if children need to use the bathroom? What activities are available during inclement weather?

Use of television   If there is a regular period for television viewing, when is it? How long? What programs are watched? Do teachers discuss the program and use it in a meaningful context? Are children required to watch television?

Daily activities/curriculum   Is there a daily plan of developmentally appropriate activities? How are children grouped? Do the staff use paper and pencil or stress interactive group activities? Are checklists used for developmental inventories? Can parents obtain copies?

Naptime   Is there a regular period for napping? How long? Who supervises the children? Are cots provided, and is the area visible and accessible? Can the parent observe? What about electronic room monitors?

Appendix C

Early Intervention Services

MAJOR TYPES OF SERVICES

The major types of services provided to young children by health, social services, and education providers can be grouped into three categories: child direct services; family support services, and training services. Services vary from agency to agency and from community to community. The categories are broad enough, however, to encompass most of the services currently being provided.

Child Direct Services

Early intervention services include those services that are necessary to meet the unique developmental needs of the child. These child direct services provide services as determined by the needs of the individual infant or toddler who is disabled. The services may include medical, education or community services, depending on the individualized family service plan for the child.

Examples of Child Direct Services include:

- Case management services that include assistance and services provided by a case manager to an eligible child and the child's family.
- Family training, counseling, and home visits that include services provided as appropriate, by social workers, psychologists, and other qualified personnel to assist the family of an eligible child in understanding the special needs of the child and enhancing the child's development.

- Health services that include services necessary to enable a child to benefit from other early intervention services during the time that the child is receiving other early intervention services.
- Medical services only for diagnostic or evaluation purposes that includes services provided by a licensed physician to determine a child's developmental status and need for early intervention services.
- Occupational therapy that includes services to address the functional needs of a child related to the performance of self-help skills, adaptive behavior and play, and sensory, motor, and postural development. These services are designed to improve the child's functional ability to perform tasks in home, school, and community settings.
- Transportation that includes the cost of travel and related costs that are necessary to enable a child and the child's family to receive early intervention services.

Other Child Direct services may include:

- In-home nursing care
- Counseling
- Specialized day care
- Recreation
- Monitoring by service providers that includes review of individual care and service plans, case management supervision, and follow-up services to ensure implementation of plans and quality services.

Family Support Services

Family support services are those services provided to the family of the child who is disabled to supplement the direct services provided to the child. The nature of these supportive services is determined by the needs of each family. Family services may include alternative living arrangements and assistance in coping with a wide variety of health, educational, and social problems.

Examples of Family Support Services are:

- Respite Care that includes the provision of temporary care for children who are disabled to provide the family time for other activities or to provide relief to the family in times of stress; it may be provided in the home or a nearby community facility.
- Homemaker Services that provide assistance to families in the care and maintenance of the home and daily housekeeping activities.
- Special Living Arrangements that include alternative community residences such as group homes or special care facilities.
- Foster Care that makes arrangements for a child to be raised by persons other than the natural or adoptive parents, until such time as other permanent arrangements can be made for the child.

- Information and Referral Services provided to families by a variety of agencies and professionals that includes answering questions, providing facts or data, and directing families to appropriate sources of community assistance.
- Counseling Services that provide discussion of options and support for families concerning a wide variety of issues and problems.
- Legal Services that involve assistance to families on legal matters, such as due process relating to parental rights, guardianship issues, and access to service.
- Case Management that applies to individual case supervision and monitoring of services provided; the family members are active participants in the process.

Training Services

Training services are educational and staff development activities provided by health, human service, and educational agencies for families of children who are disabled, for staff working with the disabled, and for the community. Training may be provided to address a variety of topics, from caring for the technologically dependent child who is disabled at home to the issue of provider liability.

Examples of Training Services follow.

- Parents and Families may include training in handling the infant and toddler's daily activities such as feeding and grooming; these activities may involve training in parental rights, or may involve training in coping with a wide variety of health, educational, and social issues.
- Aides may be involved in the initial orientation to the child; they may include alternative communication techniques; and they may address the physical care of the child with communicable diseases.
- Foster Care and Respite Care includes information and education for those individuals involved in caring for children in foster care homes or respite care arrangements.
- Inservice Training involves staff development for health, human service, and education staff. Short-term training may be given on such topics as state and federal legislation, health programs, development of individual plans, communicable diseases, and liability issues for service providers.
- Continuing Education includes professional development through educational courses that are sponsored in a manner that enables staff to obtain course credit. The topics are job related and provide professional enrichment.
- Community Awareness Activities include the use of the media for public awareness activities, such as making the public aware of a new

program or service, and also to publicize various health and educational issues.

EARLY INTERVENTION SERVICES [34 CFR 303.12]

Audiology services include:

1. Identification of children with auditory impairment, using at-risk criteria and appropriate audiologic screening techniques.
2. Determination of the range, nature, and degree of hearing loss and communication functions, by use of audiological evaluation procedures.
3. Referral for medical and other services necessary for the habilitation or rehabilitation of children with auditory impairment.
4. Provision of auditory training, aural rehabilitation, speech reading and listening device orientation and training, and other services.
5. Provision of services for prevention of hearing loss.
6. Determination of the child's need for individual amplification, including selecting, fitting and dispensing appropriate listening and vibrotactile devices, and evaluating the effectiveness of those devices.

Case management services include assistance and services provided by a case manager to an eligible child and the child's family.

Family training, counseling, and home visits include services provided as appropriate, by social workers, psychologists, and other qualified personnel to assist the family of an eligible child in understanding the special needs of the child and enhancing the child's development.

Health services include services necessary to enable a child to benefit from other early intervention services during the time the child is receiving other early intervention services.

1. The term includes, but is not limited to, clean intermittent catheterization, tracheotomy care, tube feeding, the changing of dressings or osteotomy collection bags, and consultation by physicians with other service providers concerning the special health care needs of eligible children that will need to be addressed while providing other early intervention services.
2. The term does not include services that are surgical in nature (such as cleft-palate surgery, surgery for club foot, or the shunting of hydrocephalus); or purely medical in nature (such as hospitalization for management of congenital heart ailments, or the prescribing of medicine or drugs for any purpose), devices necessary to control or treat a medical condition, or medical health services (such as immunizations and regular "well-baby" care) that are routinely recommended for all children.

Medical services for diagnostic or evaluation purposes only that include services provided by a licensed physician to determine a child's developmental status and need for early intervention services.

Nursing services that include:

1. The assessment of health status for the purpose of proving nursing care, including the identification of patterns of human response to actual or potential health problems.
2. Provision of nursing care to prevent health problems, restore or improve functioning, and promote optimal health and development.
3. Administration of medications, treatments, and regimens prescribed by a licensed physician.

Nutrition services that include:

1. Conducting individual assessments in nutritional history and dietary intake; anthropometric, biochemical, and clinical variables; feeding skills and feeding problems; and food habits and food preferences.
2. Developing and monitoring appropriate plans to address the nutritional needs of eligible children based on the findings in paragraph §F(2)(g)(i).
3. Making referrals to appropriate community resources to carry out nutrition goals.

Occupational therapy that includes services to address the functional needs of a child related to the performance of self-help skills, adaptive behavior and play, and sensory, motor, and postural development. These services are designed to improve the child's functional ability to perform tasks in home, school, and community settings, and include:

1. Identification, assessment, and intervention.
2. Adaptations of the environment, and selection, design and fabrication of assistive and orthotic devices to facilitate development and promote the acquisition of functional skills.
3. Prevention or minimization of the impact of initial or future impairment, delay in development, or loss of functional ability.

Physical therapy that includes:

1. Screening of infants and toddlers to identify movement dysfunction.
2. Obtaining, interpreting, and integrating information appropriate to program planning, to prevent or alleviate movement dysfunction and related functional problems.
3. Providing services to prevent or alleviate movement dysfunction and related functional problems.

Psychological services that include:

1. Administering psychological and developmental tests, and other assessment procedures.

2. Interpreting assessment results.
3. Obtaining, integrating, and interpreting information about child behavior, and child and family conditions related to learning, mental health, and development.
4. Planning and managing a program of psychological services, including psychological counseling for children and parents, family counseling, consultation on child development, parent training, and education programs.

Social work services that include:

1. Making home visits to evaluate a child's living conditions and patterns of parent-child interaction.
2. Preparing a psychosocial developmental assessment of the child within the family context.
3. Providing individual and family group counseling with parents and other family members and appropriate social skill-building activities with the child and parents and other family members, and appropriate social skill-building activities with the child and parents.
4. Working with those problems in a child's and family's living situation (home, community, and any center where early intervention services are provided) that affect the child's maximum utilization of early intervention services.
5. Identifying, mobilizing, and coordinating community resources and services to enable the child and family to receive maximum benefit from early intervention services.

Special instruction that includes:

1. The design of learning environments and activities that promote the child's acquisition of skills in a variety of developmental areas, including cognitive processes and social interaction.
2. Curriculum planning, including the planned interaction of personnel, materials, and time and space, that leads to achieving the outcomes in the child's individualized family service plan.
3. Providing families with information, skills, and support related to enhancing the skill development of the child.
4. Working with the child to enhance the child's development.

Speech-language pathology that includes:

1. Identification of children with communicative or oral pharyngeal disorders and delays in development of communication skills, including the diagnosis and appraisal of specific disorders and delays in those skills.
2. Referral for medical or other professional services necessary for the habilitation or rehabilitation of children with communicative or oral pharyngeal disorders and delays in development of communication skills.
3. Provision of services for habilitation or rehabilitation, or prevention of communicative or oral pharyngeal disorders and delays in development of communication skills.

Transportation that includes the cost of travel (e.g., mileage, or travel by taxi, common carrier, or other means) and related costs (e.g., tolls and parking expenses) that are necessary to enable a child eligible under this part and the child's family to receive early intervention services.

This list is not exhaustive and may include other services such as assistive technology and vision services.

Appendix **D**

Requirements for Interagency Agreements

INTERAGENCY AGREEMENTS [34 CFR PART 303, §303.523]

(a) *General.* Each lead agency is responsible for entering into formal interagency agreements with other State-level agencies involved in the State's early intervention program. Each agreement must meet the requirements in paragraphs (b) through (d) of this section.

(b) *Financial responsibility.* Each agreement must define the financial responsibility of the agency for paying for early intervention services (consistent with State law and the requirements of this part).

(c) *Procedures for resolving disputes.* (1) Each agreement must include procedures for achieving a timely resolution of intra- and interagency disputes about payments for a given service, or disputes about other matters related to the State's early intervention program. Those procedures must include a mechanism for making a final determination that is binding upon the agencies involved.

(2) The agreement with each agency must:

(i) Permit the agency to resolve its own internal disputes (based on the agency's procedures that are included in the agreement), so long as the agency acts in a timely manner; and

(ii) Include the process that the lead agency will follow in achieving resolution of intra-agency disputes, if a given agency is unable to resolve its own internal disputes in a timely manner;

(d) *Additional components.* Each agreement must include any additional components necessary to insure effective cooperation and coordination among all agencies involved in the State's early intervention program. [Authority: 20 U.S.C. 1476 (b)(9)(F)]

Appendix E

Related Federally Funded
Early Intervention Programs

A summary of early intervention-related programs includes the following:

INFANTS AND TODDLERS WHO ARE DISABLED

LEGISLATIVE AUTHORITY: Individuals with Disabilities Education Act, Part H (formerly Education for Handicapped Act)

FEDERAL ADMINISTERING AGENCY: Department of Education

TYPE OF GRANT: Formula

SUMMARY: Assistance is provided to states to (1) plan, develop, and implement a statewide comprehensive, coordinated, multidisciplinary, interagency system of early intervention services for infants and toddlers who are developmentally delayed and their families, (2) facilitate the coordination of payment for early intervention services from Federal, State, local, and private sources, (3) enhance the capacity of States to provide quality early intervention services and expand and improve existing early intervention services.

Funding under this program is limited to development and implementation of a statewide system and to facilitate the coordination of payments from various funding streams. Actual payment for direct services is limited to payor of last resort. Funding levels, based on Federal appropriation, reflect the coordination role and do not provide significant new funds.

PROGRAMS FOR CHILDREN WHO ARE DISABLED: PROGRAMS OPERATED BY STATE AGENCIES (Chapter 1 Handicapped Program)

LEGISLATIVE AUTHORITY: Education Consolidation and Improvement Act of 1981, Title 1, Chapter 1, Section 554 (a)(2)(B)

FEDERAL ADMINISTERING AGENCY: Department of Education

TYPE OF GRANT: Formula

SUMMARY: This program funds grants to States to provide special education and related services to children who are disabled from birth through age 20 in State operated or supported facilities and programs. Funds are distributed on the basis of number of children and are allocated based on a child count under a stringent eligibility definition.

SERVICES FOR CHILDREN AND YOUTH WHO ARE DEAF-BLIND

LEGISLATIVE AUTHORITY: Individuals with Disabilities Education Act, Part C

FEDERAL ADMINISTERING AGENCY: Department of Education

TYPE OF GRANT: Discretionary Grant

SUMMARY: The program authorizes funding to public or nonprofit agencies, institutions, or organizations to assist State education agencies in providing special education and related services to children who are deaf-blind from birth through age 21. Authorized services include the diagnosis and educational evaluation of children at risk of being certified as deaf-blind; and consultative counseling and training services for the families of children who are deaf-blind.

ASSISTANCE FOR EDUCATION OF ALL CHILDREN WHO ARE DISABLED

LEGISLATIVE AUTHORITY: Individuals with Disabilities Education Act, Part B

FEDERAL ADMINISTERING AGENCY: Department of Education

TYPE OF GRANT: Formula

SUMMARY: Part B of the Individuals with Disabilities Education Act mandates the provision of a free appropriate public education to all children ages 3 through 21 who are disabled and provides a timetable for serving these children. Funds are allocated on the basis of a child count. The program does not mandate services to infants and toddlers who are disabled or provide funding for those infants and toddlers served. However, these funds can be used to serve them.

Federal funds provided under this Act have never approached amounts originally authorized. Funds appropriated are only allocated based on a child count of children from age 3 through 21 who are disabled. Significant State and local appropriations have been made and will continue to be required in order to provide education and related services.

HEAD START

LEGISLATIVE AUTHORITY: Head Start Act (42 U.S.C. 9831 et seq.)

FEDERAL ADMINISTERING AGENCY: Department of Health and Human Services

TYPE OF GRANT: Formula-Discretionary Grants to local agencies

SUMMARY: The four primary components of the Head Start Program are education, social services, parent involvement, and health services. Health services include nutrition, health, and mental health services. The program serves children from ages birth through 5. Ninety percent of the children served must be from low-income families. Funds are allocated to States based on the number of children, birth through age 5, in poverty and the number of children through age 18 in families receiving Aid to Families with Dependent Children. Since 1982, at least 10 percent of the enrollment opportunities in Head Start must be available for children with handicaps and services must be provided to meet their needs.

MEDICAID

LEGISLATIVE AUTHORITY: Social Security Act, Title XIX

FEDERAL ADMINISTERING AGENCY: Department of Health and Human Services

TYPE OF GRANT: Federally Matched Entitlement

SUMMARY: Medicaid is a program which provides health coverage for low-income persons. Services are provided in those instances where all of the following conditions are met: enrolled recipient, covered service, medical necessity, and participating provider. The passage of the Federal Omnibus Budget Reconciliation Act (OBRA) of 1989 has revised eligibility requirements for this program. Similarly, the legislation revised the responsibility to provide services as determined by an Early Periodic Screening Diagnostic Treatment (EPSDT) screen. Medicaid is a significant source of funding for early intervention services. There are limitations in the number of participating providers primarily due to the levels of reimbursement.

MATERNAL AND CHILD HEALTH BLOCK GRANT

LEGISLATIVE AUTHORITY: Social Security Act, Title V

FEDERAL ADMINISTERING AGENCY: Department of Health and Human Services

TYPE OF GRANT: Block Grant

SUMMARY: Funds are provided under this program for the purpose of promoting, planning, coordinating, providing, and evaluating health services for mothers and children to age 21. Program goals include (1) to assure that mothers and children, especially those with low income or limited availability of health services, have access to quality health services, (2) to emphasize preventative measures, (3) to provide rehabilitative services to children who are blind or disabled and eligible for Social Security Income under the Social Security Act, and (4) to provide comprehensive services to children who are disabled. Among the services provided are prenatal and postpartum care, health care services (assessment, diagnosis, and treatment), prevention of substance abuse, accidents, child abuse, violence, stress, obesity, lead poisoning, and comprehensive rehabilitation services for children with special health care needs, including outreach, case management, family support, and coordination with other public and private agencies.

CHILD WELFARE SERVICES

LEGISLATIVE AUTHORITY: Social Security Act, Title IV-B

FEDERAL ADMINISTERING AGENCY: Department of Health and Human Services

TYPE OF GRANT: Formula Grant

SUMMARY: The program provides Federal assistance for public social services which are directed toward: (1) protecting and promoting the welfare of children, (2) preventing, remedying, or assisting in the solution of problems which could result in neglect, abuse, exploitation of children, (3) preventing unnecessary separation of children from their families, (4) restoring to their families children who have been removed, (5) placing children in suitable adoptive homes, and (6) assuring adequate care of children away from their homes.

Services include homemaker services, day care, individual and family counseling, and arrangements for provision of temporary child care to provide respite.

DEVELOPMENTAL DISABILITIES: BASIC STATE GRANT

LEGISLATIVE AUTHORITY: Developmental Disabilities Assistance and Bill of Rights Act

FEDERAL ADMINISTERING AGENCY: Department of Health and Human Services

TYPE OF GRANT: Formula Grant

SUMMARY: This program provides grants to States for services to persons with developmental disabilities. Eligible persons are those with a severe and chronic disability which is manifested before the person reaches 22 years of age, which is likely to continue indefinitely, which results in functional limitations in three or more areas of major life activity (e.g., self-care, language, learning, mobility, self-direction, capability for independent living and economic self-sufficiency) and which requires lifelong or extended care, treatment, or services.

States are required to select two priority areas from among the four areas as follows, with the requirement that one of the priority areas be employment-related activities. The four priority areas are (1) alternative community living arrangements, (2) employment-related activities, (3) child development activities, and (4) case management services.

ALCOHOL, DRUG ABUSE, AND MENTAL HEALTH BLOCK GRANT

LEGISLATIVE AUTHORITY: Public Health Service Act, Title XIX, Sections 1911-1920

FEDERAL ADMINISTERING AGENCY: Department of Health and Human Services

TYPE OF GRANT: Block Grant

SUMMARY: The program provides funds to States for projects to support prevention, treatment, and rehabilitation activities in the areas of alcohol and drug abuse and grants to mental health centers for mental health services. States may use funds for the following mental health services: (1) services for individuals who are chronically ill and assistance to such individuals in gaining access to essential services through the assignment of case managers, (2) identification and assessment of children and adolescents who are severely mentally disturbed and provision of appropriate services to such individuals, (3) identification and assessment of elderly individuals who are mentally ill and provision of appropriate services, (4) services to identifiable populations which are currently under served, and (5) coordination of mental health and health care services provided within health care centers.

COMMUNITY HEALTH CENTERS

LEGISLATIVE AUTHORITY: Public Health Service Act, Section 330

FEDERAL ADMINISTERING AGENCY: Department of Health and Human Services

TYPE OF GRANT: Discretionary Grant

SUMMARY: This program funds community health care centers providing primary health services to medically under-served populations. Centers provide primary health services, supplemental health services to support primary health services as appropriate, referral to providers of supplemental services, and payment for the provision of such services. Costs of services provided are adjusted based on the ability of the patient to pay. Supplemental support is provided by other Federal grants, Medicaid, Medicare, third-party providers, patient fees, State, local, and other sources.

INDIAN HEALTH SERVICE

LEGISLATIVE AUTHORITY: Snyder Act of 1921 and Indian Health Care Improvement Act

FEDERAL ADMINISTERING AGENCY: Department of Health and Human Services

TYPE OF GRANT: Discretionary Grant

SUMMARY: This program provides a direct health care delivery system, a tribal health care delivery system administered by tribes and tribal groups through contracts with the Indian Health Service and the purchase of care from nontribal providers. Services include patient care, prenatal care, postnatal care, well-baby care, family planning, dental care, immunizations, and health education services.

MIGRANT HEALTH

LEGISLATIVE AUTHORITY: Public Health Service Act, Section 329

FEDERAL ADMINISTERING AGENCY: Department of Health and Human Services

TYPE OF GRANT: Discretionary Grant

SUMMARY: Migrant health centers provide comprehensive primary health care to migrant and seasonal farm workers and their families. Programs are linked or intergrated with hospital services and other health and social services. Services provided include physicians, physicians' assistants, nurse clinicians, diagnostic laboratory and radiology services, preventative health services, and emergency medical services.

PREVENTIVE HEALTH AND HEALTH SERVICES BLOCK GRANT

LEGISLATIVE AUTHORITY: Public Health Service Act, Title XIX

FEDERAL ADMINISTERING AGENCY: Department of Health and Human Services

TYPE OF GRANT: Block Grant

SUMMARY: Funds under this program may be used for the following purposes: (1) preventive health services for the control of rodents and community and school based fluoridation, (2) preventive health programs for hypertension, (3) community based programs to demonstrate and evaluate optimal methods for organizing and delivering comprehensive programs to deter smoking and the use of alcoholic beverages among children and adolescents, (4) comprehensive public health services, (5) demonstrating the establishment of home health agencies, (6) feasibility studies and planning, and (7) services to rape victims and for rape prevention. States are permitted to transfer up to seven percent of funds received under this program for use by the State under Title V of the Social Security Act (Maternal and Child Health)

HEALTH CARE FOR THE HOMELESS

LEGISLATIVE AUTHORITY: Stewart B. McKinney Homeless Assistance Act

FEDERAL ADMINISTERING AGENCY: Department of Health and Human Services

TYPE OF GRANT: Three Discretionary Grants and One Block Grant

SUMMARY: Three programs funded as discretionary grants are health services, mental health demonstration projects, and the substance abuse program. The final component, mental health, is funded as a block grant. With the exception of the substance abuse program, all of the other programs can serve infants and toddlers.

SOCIAL SERVICES BLOCK GRANT

LEGISLATIVE AUTHORITY: Social Security Act, Title XX

FEDERAL ADMINISTERING AGENCY: Department of Health and Human Services

TYPE OF GRANT: Block Grant

SUMMARY: This program primarily provides social services to low-income persons. The program goals are: (1) achieving or maintaining economic self-support to prevent, reduce, or eliminate dependency, (2) achieving or maintaining self-sufficiency, (3) prevention or remedying neglect, abuse, or exploitation of children and adults unable to protect their own interest, (4) preventing or reducing inappropriate institutional care, and (5) securing referral or admission for institutional care when other forms of care are not appropriate.

Subject Index